Coping with Moods

YOUNG ADULT'S GUIDE TO THE SCIENCE OF HEALTH

Allergies & Asthma

Contraception & Pregnancy

Coping with Moods

Dental Care

Drug- & Alcohol-Related Health Issues

Fitness & Nutrition

Growth & Development

Health Implications of Cosmetic Surgery,
Makeovers, & Body Alterations

Healthy Skin

Managing Stress

Sexually Transmitted Infections

Sleep Deprivation & Its Consequences

Smoking-Related Health Issues

Suicide & Self-Destructive Behaviors

Weight Management

Young Adult's Guide to the Science of Health

Coping with Moods

Jean Ford

MASON CREST

Mason Crest
450 Parkway Drive, Suite D
Broomall, PA 19008
www.masoncrest.com

Printed in the Hashemite Kingdom of Jordan.

First printing
9 8 7 6 5 4 3 2 1

Series ISBN: 978-1-4222-2803-6
Hardcover ISBN: 978-1-4222-2806-7
Paperback ISBN: 978-1-4222-3000-8
ebook ISBN: 978-1-4222-9002-6

The Library of Congress has cataloged the
     hardcopy format(s) as follows:

          Library of Congress Cataloging-in-Publication Data

Ford, Jean (Jean Otto)
  Coping with moods / Jean Ford.
     pages cm. – (Young adult's guide to the science of health)
  Includes index.
  ISBN 978-1-4222-2806-7 (hardcover) – ISBN 978-1-4222-2803-6 (series) – ISBN 978-1-4222-9002-6
(ebook) – ISBN 978-1-4222-3000-8 (paperback)
  1. Affective disorders–Juvenile literature. 2. Depression, Mental–Juvenile literature. I.
Title.
  RC537.F67 2014
  616.85'27–dc23
                              2013006381

Designed and produced by Vestal Creative Services.
www.vestalcreative.com

Contents

Introduction

by Dr. Sara Forman

You're not a little kid anymore. When you look in the mirror, you probably see a new person, someone who's taller, bigger, with a face that's starting to look more like an adult's than a child's. And the changes you're experiencing on the inside may be even more intense than the ones you see in the mirror. Your emotions are changing, your attitudes are changing, and even the way you think is changing. Your friends are probably more important to you than they used to be, and you no longer expect your parents to make all your decisions for you. You may be asking more questions and posing more challenges to the adults in your life. You might experiment with new identities—new ways of dressing, hairstyles, ways of talking—as you try to determine just who you really are. Your body is maturing sexually, giving you a whole new set of confusing and exciting feelings. Sorting out what is right and wrong for you may seem overwhelming. Growth and development during adolescence is a multifaceted process involving every aspect of your being. It all happens so fast that it can be confusing and distressing. But this stage of your life is entirely normal. Every adult in your life made it through adolescence—and you will too.

But what exactly is adolescence? According to the American Heritage Dictionary, adolescence is "the period of physical and psychological development from the onset of puberty to adulthood." What does this really mean?

In essence, adolescence is the time in our lives when the needs of childhood give way to the responsibilities of adulthood. According to psychologist Erik Erikson, these years are a time of separation and individuation. In other words, you are separating from your parents, becoming an individual in your own right. These are the years when you begin to make decisions on your own. You are becoming more self-reliant and less dependent on family members.

When medical professionals look at what's happening physically—what they refer to as the biological model—they define the teen years as a period of hormonal transformation toward sexual maturity, as well as a time of peak growth, second only to the growth during the months of infancy. This physical transformation from childhood to adulthood takes place under the influence of society's norms and social pressures; at the same time your body is changing, the people around you are expecting new things from you. This is what makes adolescence such a unique and challenging time.

Being a teenager in North America today is exciting yet stressful. For those who work with teens, whether by parenting them, educating them, or providing services to them, adolescence can be challenging as well. Youth are struggling with many messages from society and the media about how they should behave and who they should be. "Am I normal?" and "How do I fit in?" are often questions with which teens wrestle. They are facing decisions about their health such as how to take care of their bodies, whether to use drugs and alcohol, or whether to have sex.

This series of books on adolescents' health issues provides teens, their parents, their teachers, and all those who work with them accurate information and the tools to keep them safe and healthy. The topics include information about:

- normal growth
- social pressures
- emotional issues
- specific diseases to which adolescents are prone
- stressors facing youth today
- sexuality

The series is a dynamic set of books, which can be shared by youth and the adults who care for them. By providing this information to educate in these areas, these books will help build a foundation for readers so they can begin to work on improving the health and well-being of youth today.

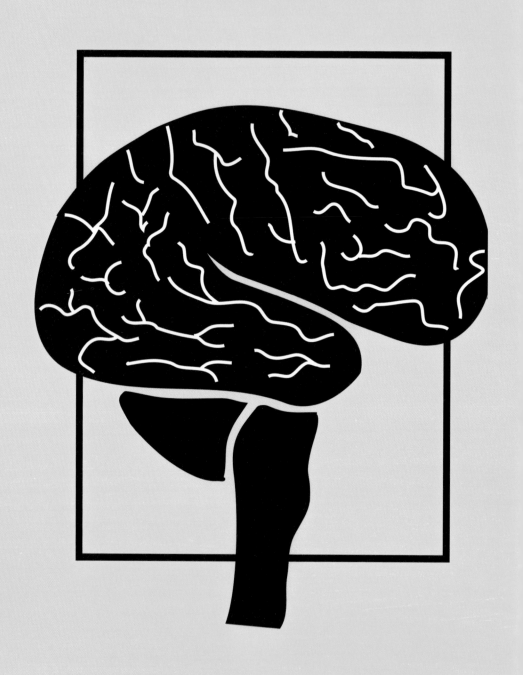

1

ROLLER COASTER EMOTIONS: The Biology of Moods

*D*ear Diary,

These days I'm a stranger, even to me. It seems like I'm either always snapping at somebody or crumpling into a pathetic, lonely heap. One minute I'm yelling and the next, crying. I'm hardly ever happy anymore, but when I am, I'm downright silly and giddy! What's wrong with me?

Have you ever felt like Jenny? Nothing is wrong with her, but going from rage to sadness to joy—all within a few minutes—can make you feel like you're losing your grip. The good news is that most teenagers experience dramatic shifts in emotion. They're normal, expected, and okay! These shifts are called mood swings.

What are mood swings? Simply stated, they are rapidly changing emotional states. They can occur without obvious cause and can range from mild to extreme shifts in emotion. Sudden changes from contentment to irritability, anger to despair, EUPHORIA to despondency, all in split seconds, are common occurrences during adolescence. So if you're experiencing something similar, know this: you're not alone.

What causes such shifts in mood? The sources vary, but for most teens, two main agents are involved: brain chemistry and life change.

Brain Chemistry

During adolescence, the same PUBERTAL HORMONES that stimulate physical changes—estrogen and progesterone in girls and testosterone in guys—also wreak havoc on your brain. Studies reported in *New Scientist* magazine and *Brain and Cognition* journal indicate that these HORMONES trigger excessive CEREBRAL activity by dramatically increasing connections between nerve endings in the brain. This activity is particularly strong in the PREFRONTAL CORTEX.

The prefrontal cortex plays a significant role in social behavior, including assessing relational cues and INTERPERSONAL self-control. How does that impact moods? Its nerve activity can become so intense during pubertal years that many teens find it hard to process basic information. This inability often leads to misinterpretation, confusion, anxiety, or feeling overwhelmed in social situations.

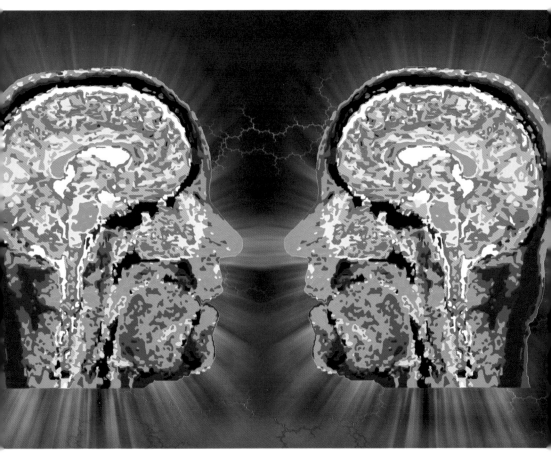

Brain activity impacts our moods and social interactions.

There's no argument that cerebral "remodeling" occurs during teen years but more research is needed to fully understand brain development. What remains undisputed is the fact that all teenagers experience FLUCTUATING mood swings during puberty.

Why exactly? Science can't answer that yet. Some researchers deny the influence of pubertal hormones on emotion. Others argue for it. Both sides agree that the brain undergoes significant development during adolescence, and mood comes down

EMOTIONAL RADAR

Three hundred adolescents, ranging in age from ten to twenty-two, were tested regarding emotional discernment. They were asked to evaluate emotions expressed in images and words. Researchers found that the speed at which subjects identified these emotions dropped up to 20 percent by age eleven, then gradually increased each year, ultimately returning to normal by age eighteen. What do these tests indicate? It seems as though a teenager's emotional radar shuts down around age eleven and is not fully operational again until he or she reaches eighteen!

to brain activity. For now it's enough to know that increased moodiness, emotional outbursts, and sudden mood swings are an inescapable part of being a teen.

Dear Diary,

I'm so frustrated! Dad's never going to let me grow up. You should have seen him this morning when I asked if I could go to Jerome's party. Ooh, there's going to be guys there. What does he think I'll do? Of course he said no, so now I can't go. How am I ever going to face everybody at school? What am I going to tell them, that I'm not allowed? Dad makes me so mad sometimes. He even had the nerve to expect a hug from "his little girl." I just stormed out and caught the bus. That's where I am now. Sorry about the bumpy writing.

Life Changes

Not only does your body change during puberty, so does your life. The way you think (the way you actually process information) and the way you interact with others (friends and family alike) constantly EVOLVE throughout adolescent years. Most teens encounter ever-changing and increasing responsibilities at home and at school. Family interactions adjust, and friendships become more complicated.

During adolescence, the brain develops in important ways that often affect emotions.

That doesn't seem fair. Adolescents must face so many new pressures while still developing the emotional and COGNITIVE skills needed to manage them. Physical maturity and all it implies is often reached years ahead of cognitive and emotional maturity. Brain remodeling is going on just as teens are encountering new and widely varying social situations. Couple those facts with the nerve-activity overload discussed earlier, and the likely outcome

Coping with Moods

is one confused, overwhelmed individual. No wonder most teens are emotional wrecks! Like ships without compasses, many adolescents are thrust into the crazy world of teen-dom without the mental tools necessary for navigating its turbulent waters.

But don't worry. The phase is only temporary. As you grow older, you develop the cognitive and PSYCHOSOCIAL skills needed to not only survive but also to thrive. Until then, accept the idea that you're stuck on an emotional roller coaster. Almost every teen is.

Just because it happens to most teens, that doesn't mean it's easy. The road ahead will be full of peaks and valleys. You'll experience moods and feelings you've never before encountered. They're countless. In his book *EQ for Everybody*, Steve Hein lists over seven hundred distinct emotions—and you're likely to encounter those seven hundred and maybe more during your teen years. Usually by age eighteen, however, radical shifts among these emotions subside.

The Anatomy of Emotions

Every emotion originates in a thought. Why is this fact so important? If we can trace our emotions back to the specific thought(s) that triggered them, and we can analyze that thought for its truthfulness or accuracy, then we might be able to impact the emotion by replacing the thought.

Here's an example. You're stuck in traffic, with an accident five miles ahead. Cars in front, alongside, and behind you are at a complete standstill. You're fuming. As you drum you fingers on the wheel, you think, *Why does this only ever happen to me?*

Analyze that scene for a moment. Cars surround you for miles! All are stuck. Each car has at least one driver; most have passengers, too. Yet you're telling yourself that this *only ever happens to you* (the thought).

COUNTLESS THOUGHTS, COUNTLESS EMOTIONS

Imagine all your thoughts on any given day. Each thought triggers an emotion. That's a lot of emotion. Here's a list of basic feelings. Try to identify thoughts that can trigger each.

accepted	cooperative	fearful
afraid	delighted	focused
aloof	dependent	foolish
angry	depressed	free
appreciated	deserving	friendly
ashamed	desirable	frozen
attractive	despondent	frustrated
belittled	determined	fulfilled
bitter	disappointed	giddy
bored	disconnected	glad
calm	discouraged	gloomy
capable	disinterested	goofy
caring	dumb	guilty
cautious	embarrassed	happy
comfortable	empty	hated
compassionate	encouraged	hateful
competent	energetic	hopeful
confused	enlightened	hopeless
connected	euphoric	hostile
content	excited	hurt

ignored	numb	supported
inadequate	obligated	tense
incompetent	optimistic	terrified
independent	overwhelmed	terse
indifferent	passionate	trapped
inferior	peaceful	trusted
injured	persecuted	trusting
insecure	pessimistic	unappreciated
inspired	pleased	unaware
insulted	proud	uncomfortable
intelligent	rejected	undeserving
interested	relaxed	ugly
intrigued	relieved	unlovable
isolated	resentful	unloved
justified	respected	unsupported
kindly	sad	unworthy
lethargic	safe	validated
lighthearted	satisfied	valuable
liked	scared	valued
lonely	secure	victorious
lost	serious	vindictive
lovable	singled out	welcomed
loved	sober	welcoming
mean-spirited	solemn	worried
melancholy	somber	worthy
motivated	squelched	wretched
needed	superior	
needy	suspicious	
nervous	stupid	

What does this thinking trigger? Feelings of indignation, injustice, an attitude of ENTITLEMENT, frustration, anger, and impatience … the list could go on and on. The more you think the thought—and most of us would sit there chewing on it over and over again—the greater the emotional intensity. Each notion feeds on the last, and anger rises. Such thinking is at best distorted, at worst, a lie. Hundreds, if not thousands, of other people are stuck in the traffic jam. How can it be happening *only to you?*

Now consider the impact on your emotions if you replaced the distorted thought with accurate thinking. *It's not just me. There must be hundreds of people stuck in this mess.* The traffic tie-up is still there, but now there's no basis for indignation or a sense of being unfairly singled out. If those emotions are absent, then anger has no foundation on which to build. Yes, you'd probably still be frustrated and even impatient—you're still stuck in traffic—but the spiraling anger would be DIFFUSED, much to your benefit and those around you.

Here's another example. Your dad asks you to do the dishes one night, but not your brother. You're furious. He never asks him to do anything. *I always have to do all the work around here. It's not fair!* Slamming the dishes into the dishwasher, you mutter, "Why do I always have to do everything?"

Look at the extreme thinking: "*never* asks him to do *anything*," "*always* have to do all the work." Is it accurate? No. Your brother was asked to unload the dishwasher the night before and to

Thoughts

create > emotions

that trigger > actions

Coping with Moods

Brooding over things often has a negative impact on your emotions.

bring in trashcans earlier that afternoon. He was also asked to clear the table while you did the dishes. Dad asks your brother to do *some* things, so obviously, your brother does work, too.

"Never" and "always" thinking is oil to an emotional roller coaster and gasoline to fiery moods. What feelings does it trigger? Much the same as those in the traffic jam scenario. Like our driver, the more you entertain such thoughts, the more you feel singled out and the more quickly you slide down the slippery slope to intense rage or anger, even jealousy or despair. Then you'll probably do—or say—something you normally wouldn't. Thoughts trigger emotions that trigger action.

Remember, if you're willing to honestly examine the thinking behind your emotions, you'll find it's often exaggerated or simply untrue. The next time you sense anger and frustration welling (or even self-criticism or hopelessness), try examining what you're thinking. You might be surprised.

Roller Coaster Survival

Now that we've discussed the anatomy of emotions, let's look at how to deal with them. Obviously the first and most effective means of controlling emotions is taking thoughts captive (before any feelings get rolling) and replacing them with accurate, rational thought, nipping the problem in the bud. That's what we just covered, but what else can a teen do? Here are ten suggestions:

1. Recognize and employ the power of your thought-life. Distorted, exaggerated, or false thinking tends to lead to unhappiness, frustration, anger, jealousy, misguided choices, false accusations, and even low self-esteem. Remember: thoughts trigger emotions that trigger actions

and words, in that order. If the thinking is wrong, the emotion is likely misguided and the pieces of your self-control will fall like dominoes.

2. Recognize the power of emotions on you. They dictate how you interact within your world. They create and permeate mood. They can also color perceptions of events and relationships ("blinded by rage") or even distort reality ("viewing the world through rose-colored glasses").

3. Recognize the power of emotions on others. Have you ever heard the saying, "When Momma ain't happy, no one is happy?" Well, the same may be true for other members of the family as well.

4. Beware of emotional reasoning. That's when we allow our emotions to lead us to faulty conclusions. "I feel it's so, so it must be true." For example, you conclude you must *be* a failure because you *feel* like a failure. Feelings cannot determine truth. They're too SUBJECTIVE.

5. Accept the fact that people are born with different temperaments. Some kids are laid back; others are high strung. Some teens never get flustered, while others fly off the handle over anything. You might be outgoing, and your best friend is shy. The way we each experience emotion—and how we manifest that emotion—is often dictated by our respective personalities. And that's okay. Go easy on yourself; work only on what you can impact.

6. Control the snowball effect. That's when we assume that because one thing goes wrong, everything will go wrong, or since one situation is overwhelming, everything is overwhelming. It's also when we begin to anticipate events, layering stressors and/or perceptions one on top

MANAGING THE PHYSICAL SIDE OF MENTAL HEALTH

- Get adequate rest: if possible, nine hours a day! (This is perhaps one of the easiest and most effective ways of managing moods.) But don't sleep too long: over ten hours can increase fatigue, lethargy, and sluggishness.
- Eat right. Avoid caffeine, high-sugar foods, and alcohol. Limit junk and fast foods. Increase your intake of proteins, fruits, and veggies. Drink lots of water: over eight glasses a day.
- Exercise regularly: at least twenty to thirty minutes of vigorous activity five days per week.
- Take a twenty- to thirty-minute nap. (No longer!)

of the other before they're even encountered. TAKE ONE THING AT A TIME!

7. Be realistic in your expectations of self and of others. No one is perfect; so don't expect perfection from others— or yourself. Shed that "superwoman" or "superman" image or you'll be CHRONICALLY disappointed.

8. Share your thoughts and feelings very specifically with someone you trust. Don't try to cope alone.

9. Journal. Analyze what you're experiencing instead of playing victim to it. Try to identify the thinking behind the emotions.

10. Take good care of your physical body.

To be human is to be feeling. The human experience is one of constant emotion. Even with the best of care, fluctuating emotions are unavoidable. Part of moving into adulthood is learning how to deal healthfully with them. In the following chapters, we'll explore the most common emotions of adolescence, their frequent causes, and the means of coping with each.

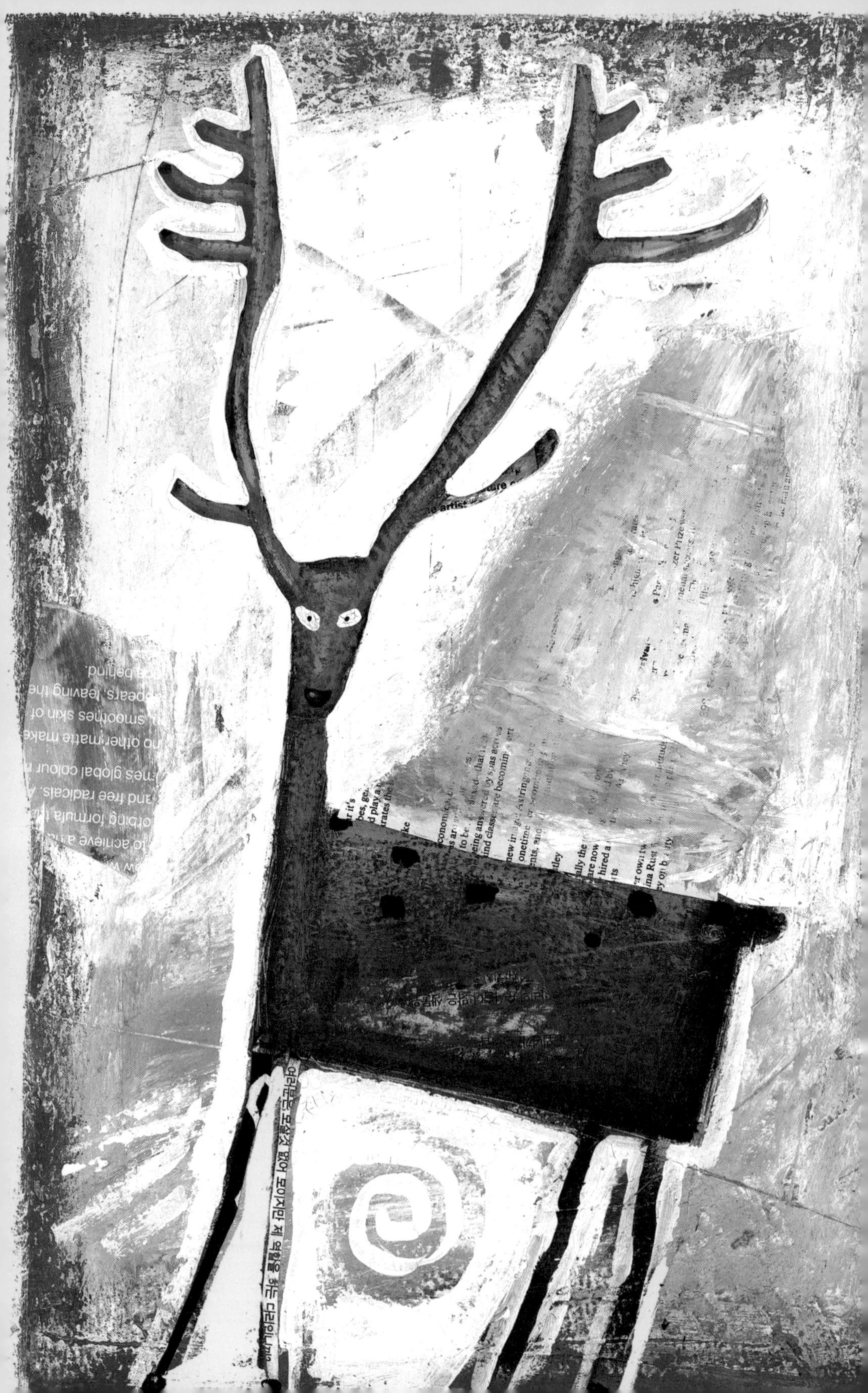

2

THE FRONT CAR:
Fear and Anxiety

Dear Diary,
     Tomorrow I start high school. How can I ever face those up-perclassmen? I still look twelve. Plus I was chosen for AP classes, so all the seniors are bound to think I'm some nerdy little kid. I'm so nervous. How will I ever fit in?

Nothing causes fear and anxiety more than the unknown. Everyone encounters new situations, so everyone experiences both of these emotions. The trick is to capture the positive value in each without succumbing to the negative.

Fear or anxiety in proper amounts can protect us from harm. Our brains use fear to caution us and make us more alert. Anxiety warns us and can make us more astute or persistent. Both

Fear can warn us to stay away from danger—but it can also distort our perceptions of reality.

Coping with Moods

are essential to physical safety—but what about psychosocial well-being?

Fear of failure can motivate. Fear of rejection can result in compromise. Fear of isolation can stimulate reaching out. Fear of dying can lead to richer living. Think about it: fear of consequences maintains safety and order in our homes, schools, and society. Even fear of the unknown has its benefits: it can cause us to take reasonable precautions and prevent us from taking foolish risks.

Anxiety has its good points, too. It can trigger self-assessment of thoughts and expectations. (Are they true? Realistic? Reasonable?) Anxiety can also motivate us to do and be our best.

Both emotions positively influence our lives. We couldn't function healthfully without them. But in excessive amounts, either emotion can distort reality. If either fear or anxiety becomes exaggerated, it can prevent us from experiencing the more positive feelings in life—such as fulfillment, victory, joy, trust, and intimacy—by leading to inaction or avoidance.

Dear Diary,

I saw her again today across the lunchroom. Mustering up every ounce of courage I had, I even headed her way. I really was going to do it this time. I really was going to ask her to the dance, but when her brown eyes looked up at mine, I froze. I just couldn't go through with it. So I pretended I was going to another table and walked right on by. What's WRONG with me? I'm such a coward. Now I'll never know if we would have clicked.

Why did this young man keep walking? Fear. Of what or whom was he afraid? What thoughts triggered his paralysis? He doesn't tell us, but we can take a guess. *I'm going to make a fool of myself....She's going to say no....She'll never go out with me...She probably thinks I'm a jerk or goofy-looking....What am I going to say? What if I fumble my words? What will her friends think? What if she says no? What if she says yes?*

In this case, fear resulted in inaction. Fear kept him from experiencing possible hurt or embarrassment, but it also prevented him from experiencing the joy, excitement, pleasure, and fulfillment he would have experienced if she had said yes. By caving in to his fear he denied himself potentially the time of his life.

But none of us will ever know what someone is really thinking or what he or she will actually do unless they choose to clue us in. No one can read minds or predict the future. You can never know with certainty what will happen—if for instance, you ask someone to do something or you try out for a team—unless you try. So stop speculating. It's futile. Plus it's emotionally draining and needlessly nerve-wracking, and only feeds fear and anxiety.

Dear Diary,

I tried out for the basketball team today. Whoa, was I scared. I've been sweating this for two weeks! To be honest, I almost didn't try out. But instead of letting my fear get in the way (like Dad said), I used it to drive me to practice hard. And guess what? I MADE THE TEAM! Woohoo! Can you believe it? It's only JV, but only a few sophomores made it at all, and I was one of them. I'm glad I didn't chicken out.

In this case, the young person used his fear of failure, plus his anxiety about how he'd compare with other candidates, to work at being the best he could be. It paid off. If he had chickened out like the other individual did, he would have never known what he could do. Plus, he would have cheated himself of feelings of accomplishment, pride, and excitement that went along with seeing his name posted on the JV list.

Just how did he overcome his concern? Again, we don't know for certain, but he may have done two things:

1. He grabbed hold of distorted thoughts that were fueling his fear and replaced them with accurate thinking.
2. He chose to utilize any remaining "negative" emotions positively by allowing them to motivate instead of defeat him.

For example, he probably initially had thoughts like *I'll never make the team.* That's common, but how he dealt with them set him apart. First, he likely caught that thought. *Wait a minute. I don't know that for sure. I'm pretty good with a basket-ball. Even though I'm only in tenth grade, other sophomores have made the team.* Do you see how deliberate grabbing hold of a thought becomes? He's literally talking to himself in his head, replacing exaggerated thinking with rational thinking.

Second, he chose to use the facts of the situation—no matter how discouraging they could be—to motivate him to do his best. *Being a sophomore hurts my chances, but I'll just practice all the harder these next two weeks to make sure I'm ready.* He could have used his circumstances to defeat himself before trying. *Why bother to try out? I'm only sophomore and sophomores rarely make the team.* But he didn't. That was his choice. It can be yours, too.

What does this individual's example teach us about fear and anxiety, and also about all emotions in general? Normal feelings in and of themselves are neither positive nor negative, neither good nor bad. They just are. They're neutral. It's how we use them that determines their benefit or detriment. Like the individuals described earlier in this chapter, it's our choice.

When Fears and Anxiety Become Abnormal

When do fear and anxiety become ATYPICAL? What's the difference between normal and not normal? How can I tell if what I'm feeling is okay?

Everyone gets anxious, uneasy, and even scared from time to time. That first day of school, final exams, new situations, starting a job, performing in front of others—all these things can make your palms sweat. You're nervous, your heart pounds, you might even feel shaky. Everyone goes through that.

However, when your anxiety or fear becomes chronic, long-term, and so serious that it interferes with your ability to function, you may be suffering from an anxiety disorder. Such disorders are the most common form of mental illness.

We're not just talking about a case of nerves here. And we're not talking about fear associated with an upcoming event(s) that dissipates as soon as it's passed, like anxiety before a test or fear of asking someone out. Everyone goes through that. (That's healthy and can be to our benefit.)

Anxiety disorders cause you to feel anxious most of the time. Everyday situations become so uncomfortable that you feel like avoiding them altogether. Or you experience recurrent instances of fear so intense they immobilize you. That kind of terror is abnormal, and the psychiatric issues can be many. For our purposes, we've lumped them into two main groups.

1. GAD—generalized anxiety disorder. Six months or more of chronic, exaggerated worry and unfounded, DISPROPORTIONATE tension characterize this disorder. It's more severe than the anxiety most people experience and interferes with normal living. You usually can't overcome this type of fear or worry through willpower or positive thinking. It has a life of its own.

A person who has an anxiety disorder feels worried and anxious almost all the time.

2. Phobias. These are unreasonable fears—note *unreasonable*—triggered by the presence (or even just the thought) of a specific object or situation that normally presents little or no real threat. Phobias, a form of anxiety, fall into three main groups:

   · Specific (or "simple") phobias: fear of specific objects or circumstances (for example, spiders, snakes, flying, heights, tight spaces). Each fear has its own name.
   · Social phobia: extreme anxiety in social or public situations.
   · Agoraphobia: fear of being in public places from which there is no readily accessed escape (for example, an elevator or crowded event).

Remember, in both phobias and anxiety disorders, we're referring to conditions that interfere with day-to-day life. That's the key measure. Everyone is afraid of something sometime, but these forms of fear are extreme. (For example, someone you know won't go to the mall or any restaurant because he or she fears using public restrooms. That fear level definitely interferes with a normal social life.)

With regard to fear and anxiety, how can you tell if you've crossed the line from moods to mental illness? Here are a few additional symptoms for which to be on guard:

   · chronically agitated or restless behavior
   · six months or more of relentless worry about things for which there are no legitimate causes for concern
   · ongoing indifference to people, circumstances, or things
   · lack of motivation, interest, or enthusiasm for things that used to excite you
   · chronic fatigue and loss of energy

PHOBIA FACTS

- Anxiety disorders (including phobias) affect as many as 18 percent of all Americans.
- Just under seven million Americans will have GAD during any given year.
- GAD affects women more often than men.
- Around 5 percent have specific phobias (snakes, flying, tight spaces, germs, etc.).
- Specific phobias usually start suddenly in adolescence or adulthood. GAD usually begins in childhood or early adolescence.
- Phobias are the most common mental illness in women and the second most common mental disorder in men over twenty-five.
- In extreme cases of agoraphobia, sufferers are afraid to leave their homes . . . and may not for years!

- sleep disturbances (too much or too little)
- disproportionate responses to circumstances (including violence)
- long-term reclusive behavior (sometimes called cocooning)
- difficulty concentrating
- falling grades
- PERVASIVE low self-esteem
- viewing small mistakes as greater than they really are
- sensing all eyes are on you all the time
- other physical symptoms can include headaches, trembling, and muscle tension.

A common phobia is arachnophobia, or fear of spiders.

Coping with Moods

PHOBIAS

We've heard of people being scared of snakes, bugs, heights, or even speaking in front of a group, but did you know that some medical encyclopedias list over three hundred specific phobias? How many of these have you heard of?

alektorophobia—fear of chickens
nephophobia—fear of clouds
acerophobia—fear of sourness
scopophobia—fear of being looked at
ablutophobia—fear of washing or bathing
lachanophobia—fear of vegetables
plutophobia—fear of wealth
xanthophobia—fear of the color yellow
acousticophobia—fear of noise
rhytiphobia—fear of getting wrinkles
bibliophobia—fear of books
peladophobia—fear of bald people
eremophobia—fear of being oneself

If you see yourself in more than one or two of these symptoms, you might be struggling with a clinical phobia or anxiety disorder. Please talk with your parents or another trusted adult. Then a licensed physician or psychologist should conduct a complete medical and psychiatric evaluation.

Most fear or anxiety disorders are easily diagnosable and can be overcome with proper treatment. Usually the course of treatment includes an antianxiety medication combined with some form of "talk" therapy. Talk therapy can include private counseling, support groups, and training in cognitive therapies.

Clinicians may help patients develop coping skills and learn to use relaxation techniques. These approaches are quite effective in managing, if not conquering fears, but treatment can only help you if you diligently apply it.

Don't try to tackle debilitating fears alone. Some teens think they can, or they try to ignore their feelings, hoping they'll go away. Psychological disorders seldom go away on their own! If left untreated, such fears worsen, chronically impeding the lifestyle of their victim. That's not healthy. We're simply not designed to sustain such ongoing stress physically or emotionally. The good news is you don't have to.

Normal but Anxious

In a study of 150 high school students reported in the *Journal of the American Academy of Child and Adolescent Psychiatry*, teens were prompted to record their feelings every half hour on specially designed hand held computers. A full 45 percent of the entries dealt with anxieties or fears. That's almost half of what these kids thought and felt! These computer "diaries" provided interesting, and sometimes surprising, insights:

- Teens with high levels of anxiety tend to spend more time alone, engaging in fewer conversations and recreational activities than low-anxiety counterparts.
- These same high-anxiety teens indicated lower levels of anxiety when they were around friends than when they were alone.
- High-anxiety teens are seven times more likely to report anger and eleven times more likely to report sadness.
- Moderate- to high-anxiety teens are two to three times more likely to smoke, yet less-anxious teens experience greater anxiety if and when they smoke.

Coping with Moods

THE FRONT CAR: Fear and Anxiety

Talking to a counselor or therapist is one treatment for anxiety disorders. This form of psychological treatment has its roots in Freud's psychoanalytic theory.

Coping with Moods

- High-anxiety teens are 70 to 80 percent more likely to drink alcohol.
- Highly anxious teens are also more likely to eat more.
- Girls are equally anxious as boys.

What does this study indicate? Clearly, chronic anxiety places you at higher risk for destructive behaviors like smoking or substance abuse. Even when fears and anxiety fall below DIAGNOSTIC THRESHOLDS or within normal ranges, the daily lives of anxious adolescents differ meaningfully from those of their peers. Normal fear takes its toll.

What You Can Do

So you're a typical teen—loads of fears and insecurities—but you wouldn't say you need professional help. What can you do to conquer your fears? Here are some ideas:

1. Acknowledge your fear. Own it. You can't deny the physical symptoms, so why deny the psychological triggers? You may find yourself denying your feelings, afraid, too, of what others will think. Don't worry about it; contrary to locker room boasts, everyone has fears. They're normal and usually healthy. Denying you're worried, concerned, or downright afraid won't help. In fact, such denial can prevent you from CAPITALIZING on the positive effects of these feelings. Accepting anxiety is the first step in conquering it.

2. Identify of what or whom you're afraid. This goes back to some of what we discussed earlier. Grab the thoughts underlying the fear. Analyze them. What's spawning the anxiety? Is your fear reasonable and/or proportionate to

MEDIA MADNESS

If movies and television reflect the human condition, then we're one scared people! See if you can match some famous "scaredy-cat" characters with their fears.

Adrian Monk (of USA's *Monk*, 2003)	Flying
Indiana Jones	Heights
Paul Vitti (in *Analyze This*, 1999)	Water
Truman Burbank (in *The Truman Show*)	Everyday tasks, his world
"Scottie" Ferguson (in *Vertigo*, 1958)	Snakes
Max Klein (in *Fearless*, 1993)	Germs, crowds, milk

(ANSWER: the fears are listed in reverse order of their characters)

the circumstances? If so, use it to your benefit. If not, adjust your thinking. Deliberately talk yourself out of it.

3. Discuss your concerns. Express them in some form. Pour your soul into a private diary if you're uncomfortable sharing thoughts aloud, or confide in a trusted friend. Sometimes he or she can offer helpful perspectives.

4. Seek advice on how to deal with that with which you're concerned. The best people to approach are those who have tackled similar issues. They've been there, can identify with you, and have had first-hand experience from which to guide you.

5. If your fears are controlling your life, seek professional help. Approach a teacher, your parents, your pastor, or another trusted adult.

Anxious feelings or chronic fears can be overwhelming or frustrating. And frustration often leads to anger. Consequently, teenagers who are more anxious than their peers are also more likely to experience angry moods. Next, we'll take a look at these common emotions.

3

Car Two:
Anger and Frustration

Dear Diary,

I can't take it anymore. Mom and Dad have total control over everything. It's so frustrating! I can't go anywhere without them driving. I hate being this dependent. It seems as though every time I ask them to drive me to Rose's or the mall or to practice, they make such a big deal out of it. "We're not a limo service," is their favorite dig these days. That really makes me mad. They just don't understand my life right now.

Shelly is fifteen going on twenty. She's not yet driving, but she wants the freedom to go and do what she pleases when she pleases. It kills her to depend on Mom or Dad for rides. That's frustrating, and it makes her angry.

Unfortunately, her anger creates fertile ground for misinterpretation. Sometimes when Shelly's parents say no, it has nothing to do with their understanding and everything to do with timing. They may just be exhausted from work, or low on gas, or maybe it's the fourth run that day and they're tired of being in the car. Whatever the reason, they may or may not communicate it—they should—but even if they do, many teens are too angry to listen.

Understanding Anger

What is anger? Anger is an emotion that can range from fleeting irritation to full-fledged rage. It is usually felt in reaction to a situation or another's actions or words. Interestingly, anger is almost always a secondary emotion. If you trace it back, it is not usually the first thing you feel.

Dear Diary,

Mom won't let me date. I can't believe it. I'm fifteen! Everyone else is dating, and I know some kids who were allowed to date when they were only fourteen. It's not fair!! Why do I have to wait till I'm sixteen? What's so magical about that number?

I guess they just don't trust me. That hurts. And it makes me mad.

Shelly's anger and Gary's anger are both rooted in frustration—frustration at their lack of control, frustration with being parented, frustration at being denied, and so on. But look at Gary's last thought. His anger was also born of feeling untrustworthy. He was first hurt, then angry.

Anger is often our response to situations where we feel hurt, frustrated, and misunderstood.

Anger most commonly follows primary feelings of helplessness or being injured, insulted, offended, violated, or denied. It can have both internal and external causes. For example, the anger you feel at helplessness in a traffic jam is from an external cause. The rage that builds from brooding over jealousy is internally prompted.

What physiological changes does anger promote? Your heart rate and blood pressure rise. In extreme cases, you flush or even tremble with rage. The levels of energy hormones like adrenaline and noradrenaline (thought to serve originally as SURVIVAL MECHANISMS) become elevated and you might even feel a "rush." But these hormones were designed to aid us in surviving short-term, physically threatening situations, and then subside. Our bodies take the toll if we remain in constant or chronic states of heightened response.

Like all emotions, anger is rooted in thought-life. Consequently, it too is neutral; the feeling itself is neither good nor bad. But anger has developed a bad reputation in our culture. Most people perceive it as negative or wrong. Why? Because most people associate the ill-conceived actions of anger with the emotion.

Positive or beneficial forms of anger frequently result from injustice. Think about that for a moment. Can you name any social changes in American history that were born of outrage? How about our independence? Abolition of slavery? Workers' rights? Equal rights? DUI (driving under the influence) and sexual predator laws? The list is endless.

Frustration and anger can be great motivators for good when handled appropriately. They aren't automatically wrong or detrimental; it's what we do with them that matters. That's the condition.

Dealing with Anger and Frustration Appropriately

Some people will tell you that the most effective way to deal with anger or frustration is to shelve it. Deny it. Pretend nothing ever happened. If you look at things from a short-term perspective, this approach may seem to make life go more smoothly—but in the long-term, unexpressed anger and frustration ultimately create more problems as they seep out in other forms. Anger will come out. It has to. Here are some of its disguises.

People who haven't learned how to constructively express their anger often tend to be highly critical. They put others down or criticize everything they encounter. They're perpetual CYNICS, often making skeptical comments regardless of any justification. Not surprisingly, they're so miserable that they aren't likely to have many successful relationships. Do you know anyone like this? Most of us do.

Unexpressed anger can also lead to PASSIVE-AGGRESSIVE expressions of what's really going on inside. For example, instead of firmly, but respectfully confronting a person head-on, you choose to retaliate indirectly, without telling him or her why. The old silent treatment is a common example of how such anger-repression is manifested. As tempting as it may be, take caution; this type of passive-aggressiveness can become vindictive and PATHOLOGICAL.

The events at Columbine High School perhaps epitomize unexpressed anger gone pathological. Eric Harris and Dylan Klebold (the shooters) allowed frustration and rage (in response to years of being bullied) to silently build until they devised a way to get even without telling their victims why. In fact, almost all school-shooters attest to dealing silently with the frustration of being outcast or bullied. The problem lies not in their circumstances, but in their silence. Repressed anger always finds a way to erupt.

Coping with Moods

FIREARM MORTALITY

Uncontrolled anger too often results in violent death, particularly in shootings. According to the National Vital Statistics Bureau, in the year 2010 alone, 30,470 people lost their lives to gunshots in the United States:

- annual firearm deaths (year 2010): 30,470
- firearm death rate per year for ages fifteen to twenty-four: 5,935
- firearm death rate per year for ages ten to fourteen: 187
- firearm homicide deaths: 11,078
- firearm suicide deaths: 19,392 (usually motivated by depression, not anger)

Anger itself is simply a feeling, not a behavior. It has many forms: irritation, frustration, indignation, resentment, revenge, rage, fury, and so on. We see and encounter the expressions of varying degrees of anger, not the emotion itself. That's an important distinction. The behavior is not the emotion; it reveals the emotion.

There are various ways in which people manifest anger. Some withdraw or brood. Others become defiant or destructive. Still others lash out with words and violence. Most want to "get back" in some fashion. That's common.

Why do we tend to desire retaliation when angry? In a nutshell, our rage is misdirected. We intellectually fail to separate people from their actions.

If you're willing to honestly examine the times when you've been really angry, you may find you're rarely angry with a person, but rather with something you or they said or did. There's a difference. It's the circumstances, words, or interactions that most often enrage us, not the human being herself. But we can't seem to separate the two.

And if we're even more honest, we'll realize that sometimes our anger is disproportionate to the events at hand. Angry responses can often be a product of the amount of sleep you've had (or not had!), how hungry you are, or some recent event that put you in a bad mood.

With so many variables, and so much at stake, it's imperative to learn how to assess, manage, and express our anger constructively.

Expressing Anger

We live in a trying world. Pain and frustration—the two most common, primary emotions behind anger—are part of navigating it. Everyone encounters trials. If they're human, they respond. Occasional angry feelings are normal. However, handling anger in socially appropriate ways is a learned behavior. We all need to become adept at assessing and directing such feelings.

Have you ever seen someone in the grasp of road rage? It might remind you of a two-year-old having a tantrum. Clearly, anyone who gets that angry is out of control. That's scary. He or she obviously hasn't matured emotionally beyond the tantrum stages of early childhood.

Young children have tantrums because they don't know what to do with their feelings. The frustration and anger are exploding inside them, but these kids can't identify these emotions yet. All they know is that the feelings are real, enormous, powerful, and need to come out. These younger members of

CAR TWO: Anger and Frustration

our society have neither the intellect nor the maturity to know how to express themselves appropriately. They're emotionally immature.

We have an advantage. We're older. Hopefully, our minds are maturing cognitively and psychosocially, equipping us more and more to handle that which makes us human—our emotions. Most of us have a choice in the matter.

The next time you find yourself becoming angry, try looking within rather than at circumstances. You might silently ask:

- What situation brought on this anger?
- Why am I angry? (Am I mad just because I didn't get my way?)
- Am I separating the person from his or her actions?
- At what am I really angry? Am I reacting to hurt, frustration, or fear? What's the primary emotion here?
- What are the thoughts behind the emotions? Are they justified and accurate? Selfish? Exaggerated?
- To whom or at what is my anger actually directed? Is that direction just?
- How am I choosing to express my anger? Is it healthy for me? Is it safe for others around me?
- Am I in control of my feelings, or are my feelings in control of me?
- Can I solve the problem in a way that shows respect for myself AND respect for the others involved?
- Am I using my anger to manipulate others?
- Am I communicating effectively? Am I communicating at all?
- Am I focusing on what I can do now, or obsessing on what's already been done "to me?"

Sometimes we feel angry in competitive situations where we feel circumstances aren't fair.

Deliberately asking these types of questions—in the midst of the feelings—can bring about awareness that leads to healthy interactions with others (awareness of others and circumstances as well as self-awareness). Be brutally honest in your assessment. Your perspective might change if you can get beyond the hurt or fear.

Even running through cognitive exercises can't guarantee you won't lose your temper. Grabbing hold of runaway thoughts in the heat of the moment takes effort, discernment, and practice. Initially, it's a very deliberate process of informed restraint, but the more you employ these techniques, the more automatic they become. As your thinking matures, the cognitive disciplines become less forced. That's just part of emotional development.

In the meantime, here are ten tips for managing anger if you find it's beginning to elude your grasp:

1. Think about the thoughts behind your anger. Correct any distortions.
2. Focus on the helplessness, hurt, fear, or frustration the other person is likely experiencing that might have caused the actions that upset you. (For example, your girlfriend wants more connection; you want more personal space. If she starts complaining about your activities, don't jump to conclusions or retaliate by calling her "the old ball and chain." Instead, listen to what's underlying her words. Maybe she just misses you. Maybe she feels unloved or second-rate.) In either case, keeping your cool while trying to focus on the other person can prevent a trying discussion from escalating into a destructive one.
3. Try to sympathize with the others involved. Compassion can calm hostility.

Coping with Moods

4. Take a deep breath and hold it, or count to ten. It's an old, common method, but it works by giving you time to think. It forces delayed response.

5. Pause and think about the whole situation before you react. Calm yourself and consider the pros and cons of possible reactions. The goal should always be constructive, not destructive.

6. Calmly express your concerns without using absolutes like "always," "never," "every," and the accusing "you" statements. (For example, instead of screaming at your parents, "You never let me do anything!" and storming off, try calmly saying, "I feel like you don't trust me when you won't let me go to the mall with my friends.")

7. Simply walk away without a word. Sometimes that's a great alternative to acting out on your anger, and it shows enormous poise and maturity.

8. Try humor (not sarcasm). Humor in response to problems is a refusal to take yourself too seriously. Yes, anger is serious, but if we're honest, it's often accompanied by thoughts and ideas that can make us laugh. Maintaining a good sense of humor can go a long way toward dissipating the intensity of your feelings.

9. Change your environment. Sometimes immediate surroundings can irritate the nerves or aggravate a situation.

10. Intelligently problem-solve. Not all anger is misplaced. Legitimate difficulties or conflicts often trigger frustration and outrage. Assess the problem. Think about means of coping as a compromise to finding solutions that may not exist.

Anger can be either a powerful tool or a destructive weapon. If anger controls your life, you may need to seek help. Anger management teaches techniques for dealing constructively with anger.

Coping with Moods

Responses in tense situations can range from walking away to talking things over, from firmly expressing your anger to letting it go because you realize it's unproductive in a specific instance. Whatever the means, if you try to follow these steps whenever you can, you'll find out that anger can become a positive and productive emotion. You might even realize unexpected perks. You'll certainly feel less stress.

If you choose to express your anger, remember that it may hurt others or make the situation even worse. Restraint and discernment are keys to unlocking anger's benefits. Express feelings honestly and assertively, but not aggressively. Clarify your needs to yourself (and to others, when appropriate) and how to get them met without hurting anyone. You don't have to be demanding, demeaning, or pushy. Assert yourself with restraint and respect.

When kept in check, anger can be a powerful tool. It can motivate and inspire exceptional achievements, great athletic performances, or social advancements. It can be a means through which we grow and better ourselves. Destruction or construction: anger can result in either. You choose.

Angry People

The National Mental Health Association (NMHA) states that, "People who are easily angered generally have what some psychologists call a low tolerance for frustration, meaning simply that they feel they should not have to be subjected to frustration, inconvenience, or annoyance." Unfortunately, however, we're all subject to irritants every day. No one is spared. They're part of life.

Learning to take things in stride intellectually is critical to mental health. Logic defeats anger. If you're naturally a "hothead" like the people we just described, try using hard logic on

WORTH REPEATING

"Nothing gives one person so much advantage over another as to remain cool and unruffled under all circumstances."
  —Thomas Jefferson

"Speak when you are angry, and you'll make the best speech you'll ever regret."
  —Lawrence J. Peter

"The events of the world don't make you angry. Your 'hot thoughts' create your anger. Even when a genuinely negative event occurs, it is the meaning you attach to it that determines your emotional response."
  —Dr. David Burns

"You can't stay mad at somebody who makes you laugh."
  —Jay Leno

yourself. Do this each time you feel anger rising. You might find you have a more balanced and rational perspective.

Do I Need Help?

If anger is controlling you, if it often monopolizes your thoughts, if it's negatively impacting relationships and other important aspects of your life, you should probably consider consulting with a psychologist or other licensed, mental health professional. You definitely need help if your anger prompts violent outbursts or sustained ideas of hurting others or yourself.

Anger management can become a reality! Long-term coping mechanisms are easily learned over a relatively short time span. Psychologists claim that most highly angry individuals can dramatically improve within just eight to ten weeks of therapy; this, of course, depends on personal circumstances and actual techniques employed.

What happens in counseling? Sessions usually include a spectrum of cognitive therapies that impact thinking and behavior. They work only if you want the help and are willing to apply them. Sometimes medication is also required.

Remember, unhealthy anger can be destructive. No one can sustain it for long without negative consequences. Get help if you need it. There's a world of assistance out there just waiting to teach you how to handle your emotions. Go for it.

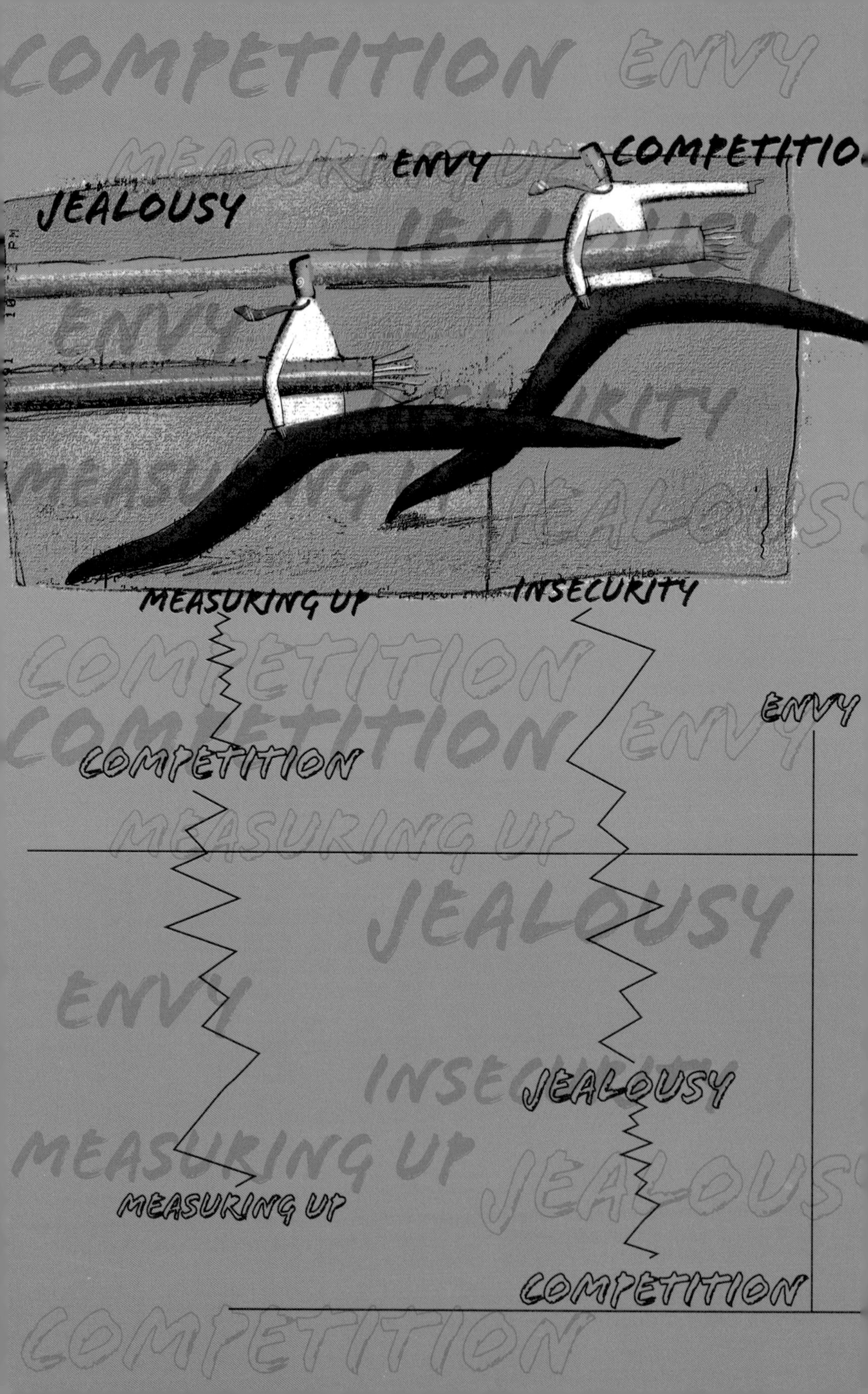
JEALOUSY
ENVY
COMPETITIO
MEASURING UP
INSECURITY
COMPETITION
ENVY
JEALOUSY
MEASURING UP
COMPETITION

4

Car Three:
Envy and Jealousy

Dear Diary,

Why did I have to get my mother's thighs? Every time I stand on the starting blocks next to Brianna, I feel enormous. She has those petite yet muscular quads that look good in a racing suit. Then there's me—thunder thighs! No matter how hard I work out, no matter how many leg presses I do, my upper thighs still jiggle. Yuk. They're so gross. I wish I had her legs.

Everyone encounters feelings of envy or jealousy some time. As with other feelings discussed in this book, these emotions are neither negative nor positive in themselves. How we deal with them becomes the ultimate judge. Our actions define their character.

Understanding the Emotion

First, let's distinguish between envy and jealousy. We often confuse the two, but they're actually different emotions that are likely to trigger different actions.

Envy is more a wishful longing for the things or traits of another. Like Dana, the feeling is usually wistful, innocent, and almost always harmless. In fact, it's often fleeting, the product of momentary discontent.

Jealousy is another creature all together. It's usually born of deep fear: fear of losing affection, esteem, status, or position. Sometimes this type of fear is so deeply embedded we don't realize that's what's driving us at all. The feeling is intensified when our loss is perceived to be to another person.

Jealousy is rarely innocent once it takes root. It's destructive, motivated by self-interest, and almost always vindictive. It grabs hold of a person and festers, becoming bitter, resentful, angry, obsessive, or full of disdain. If envy is a daydream, jealousy is the nightmare.

Dear Diary,

I can't believe Levi got the lead. I was so much better than he was at auditions. Everybody was! It's not fair. Just because he's the director's favorite, he got the role. That was my part! All I can say is that he better enjoy it while it lasts. Andy, Saul, and I already started a rumor that Levi's dealing. We even planted two nickel bags in his locker. That'll get him kicked out of drama for sure! And guess who's his understudy?

Coping with Moods

We all feel envious of others sometimes—but when envy turns to jealousy, it can become a destructive emotion that takes over our lives.

CAR THREE: Envy and Jealousy

65

In our opening example, the young woman was experiencing envy. She merely longed for something she didn't have. Her feelings originated in dissatisfaction with a part of her body. That's common and innocent.

In the young man's case, he's not just wistfully wishing for a role in the school play. He's bitterly resentful of Levi's success. He sees Levi as the person responsible for keeping him from the position of esteem he fears living without. In his mind, he lost his status to Levi. It's personal. That's jealousy at its best—or worst.

Do you see how feelings can distort circumstances? It never occurs to the young man that maybe Levi really is better than he. Or that maybe the drama coach looks at attitude and grades, too, not just at performance. This individual is blinded by his jealousy. It's consuming him. He's so worried about losing the prestige of "male lead"—especially to Levi—that he's willing to take irrational, self-centered steps to secure the status Levi was awarded.

The young woman was motivated by discontent. The young man was motivated by fear and resentment. The young woman's concern focused more on her own perceived inadequacies. The young man's target was all Levi. The young woman's observations were grounded in truth. The young man's mind wouldn't embrace reality. Envy and jealousy really are two different animals.

Unchecked envy arouses jealousy. Unchecked jealousy can become so intense that it colors almost everything a person thinks, feels, and does while in its clutches. Hence its nickname: the green-eyed monster. This monster distorts reality much like fear and anger. Jealous individuals usually see themselves as short-changed (even if they aren't) or entitled to something they may not have. Their thoughts are exaggerated; their perspective is skewed. And they are filled with bitter rage.

ENVY AND JEALOUSY DEFINED

ENVY: 1) Discontent aroused by a desire for the possessions or qualities of another.

JEALOUSY: 1) Envious or resentful of the good fortune or achievements of another. **2)** Fearful or wary of losing one's position or situation to someone else, especially in a sexual relationship. **3)** Having to do with or arising from feelings of envy, apprehension, or bitterness.

Source: *The American Heritage Dictionary*

Lacking the cognitive and psychosocial maturity to deal with such emotional intensity, teens often act on impulse. They're shortsighted. The young man in our diary entry could only see as far as getting back on stage. He never paused long enough to assess his thoughts or consider long-term consequences of his actions. If jealousy is at the root of an issue, such impulsive behavior is almost always destructive and can be criminal.

- In Maryland, a fifteen-year-old is strangled by a basketball buddy, age seventeen. The reason? The buddy wanted his friend's new Air Jordan sneakers.
- A tenth-grader is shot for his new Nikes.
- In Baltimore, a nineteen-year-old is robbed of his $40.00 sweatpants and then killed.

Teens often measure their clothes, their shoes, even the way they walk, against each other.

Coping with Moods

- Four girls ages thirteen to fifteen stalk and fatally stab a fifth girl in New Mexico. Why? She was attractive, well liked, and happened to be dating one of the killers' ex-boyfriends.
- A nineteen-year-old is fatally shot in the back when he refuses to give up the Cincinnati Bengal jacket he's wearing. The fifteen-year-old triggerman shoots him right through the "A" in "Bengals."
- Shots echo in a hallway of a junior high when a fourteen-year-old is killed for his blue, silky Georgetown jacket.
- A cheerleader's mom is found guilty of soliciting the murder of the mother of her daughter's junior-high-school cheerleading rival. She thought that if her daughter's rival's mom were murdered, then the girl would be too distraught to compete.

Extreme as they are, these crimes are true crimes. Each and every case was motivated by rampant jealousies. When unrestrained, it's frightening how far our feelings can take us. After reading about cases like these, we can't deny the power of jealousy or the necessity of learning to manage it.

Managing the Emotion

Like we discussed in earlier chapters, managing any emotion—including jealousy and envy—comes down to controlling thought-life. In this case, it's helpful to isolate your feelings and determine if you're just envious or truly jealous. The chart on the next page should help.

Where do you fall? If you struggle with envy, try to focus on what you have rather than what you don't have. Keep a "blessings" journal. List at least five things daily for which you're thankful.

ENVY	JEALOUSY
wistful want	driving need
mild and often fleeting	intense and sustained
originates with discontent	originates with fear of loss
views the other as fortunate	views the other as interfering or a threat

You'll be amazed at how content you'll start to feel. Your moods will soar.

Next, analyze the things for which you long. Are they even possible? For example, I'd love to have a long slender neck, but no amount of wishing will make that happen. I'm stuck with my neck as is. Even so, being human I still occasionally catch myself focusing on what I lack, longing for the impossible. When I do, I have a choice. I can use that longing to beat myself up, make me feel inferior, and lower my self-esteem—or I can let go of things I can't impact and begin working on that which I can.

That's where deliberate mind work comes in. Ask yourself if the object of your desire is obtainable. Be realistic. If so, use envy to motivate you instead of feeling sorry for yourself. You may not be able to grow taller, but you can work with the body you have and get it into its best form. You may not be able to move to a better neighborhood, but you can work and save toward the expensive items you crave.

Do you wish you could have those hundred-dollar sneakers? Get a part-time job and save for them. How about a certain hair

Coping with Moods

color? Get a dye job. Are you dissatisfied with your weight and wish you could be more fit like your best friend? You can. Start working out and watch what you eat. Use your envy constructively.

Too often envy becomes an excuse, and we use it to defeat ourselves before we even try. "I'll never be as talented as he is, so why try out?" "Her college will never accept me so why even apply?" That's using envy destructively. Again, you can choose how to apply your emotions.

What of jealousy? If we've already allowed a seed of envy to take root and blossom into full-fledged jealousy, is there any turning back? Of course there is, but it's not easy. This process, too, involves intentional rethinking, but you have to want to change your thoughts.

Jealousy never goes away by itself. If anything, it usually festers, taking on a life of its own. You must be willing to yank it back into place and regain control. But sometimes, if we're honest, it feels good to let jealousy thrive, so we let it be. That's dangerous.

If you find that jealousy is starting to monopolize your thoughts, take deliberate action. These ten strategies might help:

1. STOP. You can choose to stop runaway thoughts. It's a choice you can make. Pause for a moment, take a deep breath, get a grip, and carefully examine where your head is going.
2. Try to follow all thoughts to their logical outcome. (Resist the temptation to dwell in the present feeling.) Is the likely destination constructive or destructive for ALL concerned? Can anyone be hurt?
3. Analyze the steps that led you to this point. How did you get here? Have your feelings been based on true, accurate,

JEALOUS VILLAINS OF FILM AND LITERATURE

- Cain (jealous of Abel)—the Bible

- Iago (jealous of Cassio)—*Othello*

- The Queen (jealous of Snow White)—*Snow White and the Seven Dwarves*

- The stepsisters (jealous of Cinderella)—*Cinderella*

- Commodus (jealous of Maximus)—*Gladiator*

- Alex Forrest (jealous of Dan Gallagher's wife and family)—*Fatal Attraction*

and complete thoughts? Or have they been based on exaggerated perceptions, incomplete information, false ideas, or thinking that's way out there? If it's the latter, correct your thoughts. Replace them with what's reasonable and true. Be deliberate about it.

4. Identify the underlying fear. Is it rational? (For example, can you really lose your Dad's love to your brother? Can you really lose your reputation as an outstanding student to a rival, especially when you still have straight A's?) If the object you fear losing can't actually be lost, jealousy has no basis.

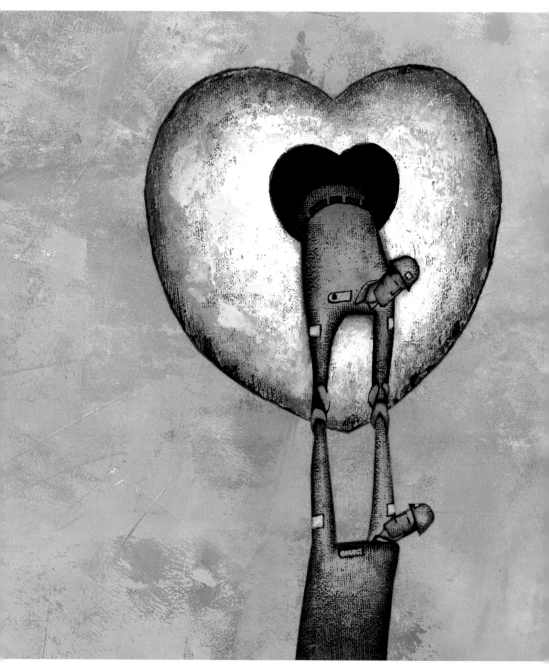

Sometimes the key to overcoming a negative emotion is to talk things over with another person. Don't be embarrassed to ask for help when you need it!

Coping with Moods

5. Force yourself to put things in perspective. How important will this desire be one year from now, five years from now, even ten years from now?
6. Consider all the consequences of all possible actions. Look long term as well as short term.
7. Think before you act. Resist impulsivity. Down the road, you'll be thankful you did.
8. Be honest about your emotions. Get them out on the table. Hiding or denying them just increases their intensity and impedes objectivity.
9. Diligently seek another's perspective.
10. If you sense jealousy is consuming you, or you have thoughts of doing something drastic, get help now.

Self-Esteem

Self-esteem, or lack of it, may play the starring role in envy and jealousy. What is self-esteem? Simply said, it is the value or sense of appreciation a person places on his or her own attributes, qualities, and character. It involves how much worth or importance that person ascribes to these traits. Frequently, it is the result of comparing what we actually see in ourselves against what we'd like to be or accomplish.

The problem with establishing self-esteem with such measures lies in the fact that too often what we "actually" see isn't actual at all. Our view is frequently exaggerated for any number of reasons. (See chapter 1.) Keep in mind that such distortions can work both ways. The kid who exaggerates his importance is arrogant and smug; he thinks he's better than everyone else. That's exaggerated. Then there's the teen who feels inferior, convinced that he has nothing to offer. That, too, is exaggerated. It's hard to be objective when it comes to yourself.

Some teens have a harsh inner critic—that voice inside that finds fault with everything they say or do. If constant criticism from others can harm self-esteem, constant criticism from within is devastating to it. A healthy self-esteem cannot grow in such an environment.

Where does this inner critic come from? Sadly, it is often modeled after a critical parent, teacher, or other adult figure whose acceptance was really important to us when we were young. The good news is that that was then—and this is now. The critic now belongs to you and can be restrained if you choose to restrain him. You can be the one to dictate what, how, and when the inner critic gives feedback. Decide right now that he will only provide constructive feedback.

Although teens often feel inadequate physically, intellectually, or emotionally, you need to distinguish between what you can change and what you can't. Work only on what you can impact. Identify any unrealistic self-expectations. Aim for improvement, not perfection.

If all you can see are your shortcomings, force yourself to think about other more positive traits that you possess. Maybe you're not valedictorian or tall, but you're pretty good at painting or playing the guitar, and you make a great friend. Each and every person has something to offer. Every teen does something right. So do you.

We said that envy is born of discontent—and discontent thrives on low self-esteem. If envy leads to jealousy, then we need to learn to build self-esteem if we hope to conquer jealousy in our lives.

It's never too late to build self-esteem. In some cases, the help of a trained, professional counselor is needed to undo past emotional hurts that could be getting in the way, but more often than not, anyone can improve his or her self-esteem. Recognizing who you are is a great first step.

Coping with Moods

Learning what can hurt self-esteem (and avoiding it) and what can build self-esteem (and applying it) are essential elements to improving how you feel about yourself. It takes a little effort, but the payoff is huge. Here are a few esteem-builders you can try:

- Focus on what you're good at and build up those abilities.
- Share what you're good at with others. (If you're a good friend, be a friend. If you're awesome at guitar, play for everybody just for fun. Consider tutoring in a subject in which you excel, or coach someone!)
- Try to force yourself to remember that self-esteem involves much more than physical appearances. Don't overlook inner qualities in yourself and others.
- Each day jot down (anywhere) three things about yourself that make you happy, pleased, or proud.
- Lose the perfectionist. The quicker the better.
- Acknowledge your accomplishments. (Hey, you didn't fail the math exam. That's great!) Take pride in new skills learned. (That first skateboarding trick, driving, even cutting your own hair!)
- Try to grab any negative thoughts about yourself before they get too far. When you catch yourself thinking like that—and you will—counter the thoughts with something positive, or at least more accurate, about yourself.
- Have fun! Enjoy spending time with the people you like and doing the things you love.

So what exactly is the payoff? Improved self-esteem plays a role in almost everything you do. You'll do better in school and enjoy it more. Relationships—with teens and adults alike—will improve, and you'll find it easier to make friends.

Healthy self-esteem will help protect you against those "left-out," jealous feelings we all get once in a while.

With healthy self-esteem, you'll find it easier to deal with mistakes, disappointments, hurts, and failures. Plus, you'll find that you're more likely to persevere and stick with something until you succeed. Physically, you'll feel better and be happier overall. Last, but not least, you might even find yourself content with your life the way it is. And that will nip envy and jealousy in the bud. The benefits are countless.

Conclusion

Many teens (and adults, too) believe the lie that worth is defined by things or appearances. Value as human beings mistakenly becomes inseparably linked to a name on a tag, a body type, on whose arm you cling, or status and position. That's sad.

Go back a minute. If you look more closely at the crimes we cited earlier, what was actually prized? Most of the assailants weren't just stealing shoes, pants, or jackets. They were taking someone else's status for their own.

Remember the cheerleading mom? She wanted recognition and prestige for her daughter, and she was willing to kill to get it. That adult mom was once a teen, but tragically, she never learned to manage her envy, fears, and jealousy. She never matured enough to realize worth has nothing to do with status or possessions. Don't make the same mistake. You're of immeasurable value just the way you are.

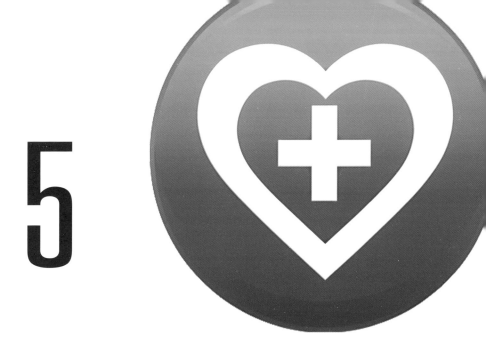

5

CAR FOUR:
Stress and Sadness

Dear Diary,
    I want to scream! Everybody needs something from me! Mom and Dad want me to watch Amy and Richard this weekend. Caroline needs me to practice her lines with her after school Friday afternoon. Exec Council expects me to help with dance decorations. And my coach said that if I miss another practice, I can't play in the next two games! Then there's homework, midterms, piano, my job, my chores, Roger's birthday.... I feel like I'm going to explode!

Poor Wendy. She's got way too much going on. Too many demands and too much pressure can result in only one thing: stress. Look closely between the lines of Wendy's journal. You'll see the stress there.

If you're feeling stressed out, you're not alone. Stress affects everyone: your friends, your parents, your neighbors, even your teachers. If you have any doubt, think back to how many times you've heard expressions like "I'm stressed out," or "I'm really under a lot of pressure right now," or "That's way too stressful." Stress is natural to life.

What Is Stress?

Frankly, stress is hard to define because it means different things to different people. Most would agree, however, that stress could be defined simply as a state of tension or pressure. When the human body encounters a situation it perceives as challenging, threatening, scary, overwhelming, dangerous, or even foreign, the body rises to the challenge with a BIOCHEMICAL reaction known as the stress response.

The stress response produces a flood of hormones that have specific physical effects. Working properly, this response maximizes a person's focus, strength, stamina, and alertness.

When the brain senses a stressor, the HYPOTHALAMUS signals the ADRENAL GLANDS to produce lots of adrenaline and cortisol (stress hormones). These hormones flood the bloodstream and travel to many areas of the body, triggering all sorts of physical changes. Blood vessels widen to let more hormone-laden blood flow to large muscle groups, resulting in increased strength. Pupils dilate to improve vision. The liver releases stored glucose (sugars) to increase the body's energy. These hormones also increase heart rate, breathing rate, METABOLISM, and blood pressure.

Coping with Moods

All these physical changes help a person rise to meet stressors by maximizing her ability to fight or flee. Fight-or-flight, as these abilities are commonly known, is the instant and automatic response in every human that alerts you to a threat while instantly preparing you to take action if need be. Fight-or-flight is necessary to primitive physical survival. But living in modernized, WESTERN CIVILIZATION has eliminated most physical threats. How does fight-or-flight work now?

Stress can be caused by all kinds of situations. Taking an important test is just one example.

Stress can trigger adrenaline reactions that impel us to achieve amazing feats beyond our normal abilities.

Coping with Moods

The fight-or-flight response takes control in modern emergency situations, like when you slam on your brakes to avoid hitting the car that just pulled out in front of you. That's the rush you feel. More often we sense a milder form of it as we face far less dramatic stressors.

You might experience sweaty palms and a pounding heart when you stand in front of the class to give your oral report, or when you step up to the free-throw line for that tie-breaking shot. You might also experience these symptoms when you sit down to midterms or find yourself face-to-face with the hottest guy on the football team. That's your stress response kicking in, preparing you to react quickly and effectively in a high-pressure situation. It's doing its job.

Why all this talk about stress responses in a book on moods and emotions? Our stress response was designed to handle *brief, immediate* situations. When the feeling of danger passed, the nervous system returned to normal, ready to respond again when needed. The problem is that stressors have changed over time and our bodies haven't.

Many stressors today are ongoing or chronic, like school responsibilities. When stressors are continuous, the stress response continues, denying your nervous system the opportunity to return to its normal state. It remains slightly activated, producing and distributing extra stress hormones for extended periods of time. Such long-term activity is hard on the body. It actually weakens the body's immune system, wears out its reserves, and leaves a person feeling depleted and overwhelmed.

That's where mood comes in. Pressures that are too intense for too long result in something called stress overload. Normal teens experiencing stress overload are more prone to emotional outbursts and may feel emotionally erratic, tense, or irritable. (This is on top of mood swings!) They often feel rushed and can get downright snippy. Talk about moody!

Time is a limited commodity. Trying to fit too much into each day can lead to chronic stress.

Coping with Moods

Anxiety-ridden teens may become worse when under chronic stress. Their fears may intensify or their worries build and become debilitating. Others become so overwhelmed that they want to cry or shut down completely. Many find themselves sad or depressed. (We talk more about sadness and depression shortly.)

Chronic stress is good for no one. It threatens health and well-being. Clearly, we need to get a grip on how to deal with the stress in our lives.

Getting a Grip

Managing stress works best when applied regularly, not just when the pressure is on. Taking control while things are relatively orderly and calm will go a long way in challenging, more frantic times ahead. Here are a few tips to help you keep stress under control:

1. Learn to say NO. Minimize stressors by cutting back on your activities. Over-scheduling is a major source of stress for teens.
2. Schedule "down time." Make it a priority. Write it on your calendar if you have to and then guard that time zealously. Get plenty of sleep (eight or nine hours nightly).
3. Exercise regularly: twenty to thirty minutes daily, five days a week. (Note: excessive exercising contributes to stress.)
4. Eat well. (Under stressful conditions, the body needs the right nutrition.)
5. Surround yourself with optimistic and positive people.
6. Don't procrastinate. Solve daily little problems as they occur. Avoiding them or allowing them to build up just adds stress.

7. Manage your thought-life. Watch what you're thinking. Your attitude and outlook impact the way you react to stressors more than you know.

8. Learn to relax. Pause. Deliberately slow down. Make time for activities that are calming and pleasurable for you (for example, listening to music, spending time with a pet, soaking in a bath).

9. BREATHE! Sounds simple, right? But most of us don't know how to breathe for relaxation. Try this: Breathe in through your nose (mouth closed) for a slow count of four, pause and hold your breath comfortably for a few more seconds, then exhale slowly through slightly parted lips for a count of eight. Repeat three or four times.

Although we most often think of stress as resulting from negative circumstances, stress is also triggered by change, excitement, or anticipation—good or bad. Any situation that requires a person to adapt to new conditions creates stress: the first day of school, being in a competition, running for student council, playing in a concert, or going to the prom. This kind of pressure can motivate you to be your best. That's good!

As long as stress remains manageable, a little can help you go a long way. But what happens when the pressure becomes unmanageable? Sometimes sadness, feelings of being overwhelmed or defeated, and depression can set in.

Dear Diary,

I just blew! Here's what happened. Mom, Dad, and I are all getting ready to go to church this morning. I'm leading a small group today—and I knew David was going to be there, so I was all stressed out about my clothes and hair. And Mom says I look cute. CUTE! I didn't say a word. Then Dad comes in and wants to know how his "little" girl is doing. I couldn't stand it any more. I exploded. I told him I wasn't a baby

A MATTER OF PERSPECTIVE

Have you ever noticed how some people seem to always take things in stride? Nothing fazes them. Doesn't that drive you crazy? What's their secret? Researchers have identified common qualities that make these people so resilient.

- They view change as a challenge and as normal.
- They see setbacks and problems as temporary and solvable.
- They view challenges as opportunities.
- They take action as soon as problems crop up.
- They believe they'll succeed if they persevere toward their goals.
- They regularly participate in relaxing and fun activities.
- They make and keep commitments to family and friends.
- They have a support system.
- They're not afraid to ask for help and do.

anymore and to stop treating me like one. I don't know why I got so mad. They were trying to be nice. All I know is that I stormed up here, slammed my door, and burst into tears. Something's got to be wrong with me.

Sadness and Depression

As teens near adulthood, they're faced with many changes. Their bodies are changing, as well as their relationships, their responsibilities, even their sense of identity. Now throw in the

Changes in your life, stress, and other pressures can lead to sadness and depression.

Coping with Moods

normal commitments, school pressures, and over-scheduling many American teens try to manage. That's a lot of pressure.

Many teens are simply overwhelmed by it all. So it's not unusual for young people to occasionally experience "the blues" or feel "down." Chronic changes and pressure can do that to you. It's normal and common.

The trick is to try to manage these feelings before they evolve into more prolonged or serious depression. Here are a few suggestions:

- Ask a trusted adult for help. Don't try to handle too much alone.
- Make and nourish a few good friendships.
- Join a club or organization geared specifically to adolescents.
- Participate in a few, well-suited school activities. (Don't overdo.)
- Analyze and alter the thoughts that are making you feel this way.
- Journal. (Writing helps you organize and express your thoughts so they become more manageable. Don't worry about grammar, spelling, punctuation, or neatness. What matters is getting the feelings out.)
- Adjust any unrealistic expectations (of yourself, your family, and your academic and social "success"). Let go of the perfectionist in you.

But despite the best of these efforts, some teens still can't shake feeling "down." When sadness, LETHARGY, and indifference persist for weeks or longer, and they begin to interfere with daily life, CLINICAL DEPRESSION may be the cause.

Dear Diary,

I'm worried about Leslie. Something's going on with her. Last Saturday she turned down a trip to the mall! Not because she had anything else to do—she just wanted to sleep in. What's up with that? She loves to shop.

Then get this—little miss brain-i-ac (she always beats me on grades) gets a D on our algebra test. A "D!" It's the first time ever that I did better than she did—and she doesn't seem to care. And then there's biology! She still hasn't turned in the lab report that was due last week.

And then the eating thing. Leslie hasn't touched lunch in weeks. She wouldn't even taste the Doritos I bought her yesterday, sort of as a test. (They're her favorite.) She claimed she just didn't have much of an appetite.

You know what the kicker is? Leslie doesn't even I.M. anymore. Used to be we would spend hours online every night. She's the only person I know who has over 100 people on her buddy list—and now she's not

TEENS AND SUICIDE

- Suicide is the third leading cause of death for young adults ages ten to twenty-four.
- Each year almost 5,000 young people ages fifteen to twenty-four kill themselves.
- The rate of suicide for young adults this age has tripled since 1960.
- In almost 50 percent of all suicides, substance abuse is a factor.
- Eight out of ten suicidal persons give some sign of their intent.
- Ninety percent of suicidal people have some form of mental disorder; 75 percent of the people who commit suicide suffer from depressive disorders.

chatting with one of them. Everybody else is chatting with everybody. What else do you do on a school night? Something's seriously wrong.

If I try to talk to her about it, she just tells me she's "not in the mood." Maybe I should mention something to her mom or dad. They're cool. I bet they've noticed something, too. I don't know what else to do.

Many factors can contribute to being depressed. Stress is one, yes, but there are other factors that could be involved: insufficient or excessive levels of brain chemicals, specifically NEUROTRANSMITTERS, other medical conditions, chronic stress, thinking patterns, abuse, neglect, trauma, and even life events like death, divorce, discrimination, and moving.

Depression is important to identify and treat because of its potentially devastating consequences. Teens suffering with various forms of depression often struggle academically. They also isolate themselves. Relationships with family and friends suffer as the person slowly withdraws. Obviously, it's critical that we learn to distinguish between blue moods and actual depressive illnesses.

How can we discern the difference between gloomy moods and clinical depression? Start by remembering that everyone gets down once in a while. These times are usually isolated and often in response to something going wrong. For example, you come home feeling dark and depressed because you had a fight with a friend or you failed a test. Sometimes blue feelings can last a bit longer and still not be considered clinical depression. This could happen when a close friend moves away and you feel their absence, or a pet dies. These feelings are all perfectly normal and eventually wane.

When feelings of sadness, worthlessness, despair, and indifference become intense and last more than two weeks, that person is considered to be clinically depressed. These feelings

Coping with Moods

DETERMINING DEPRESSION

Sometimes it's hard to tell a case of the blues from a more serious depressive disorder. The following symptoms are widely used for diagnosing clinical depression. When someone has five or more of these symptoms for two weeks or longer, they're probably depressed.

- frequent sadness, tearfulness, or crying
- prolonged (more than two weeks) sadness or blue moods
- feelings of hopelessness
- feelings of guilt or worthlessness
- withdrawal from friends and activities
- lack of enthusiasm or motivation
- decreased energy and/or lethargy
- indifference and/or disinterest
- significant changes in sleep patterns
- significant changes in eating habits
- weight gain or weight loss
- frequent physical complaints like headaches and stomachaches
- inability to concentrate or forgetfulness
- indecision
- increased agitation, irritability, anger, or hostility
- overreaction to criticism or failure
- suicidal thoughts

Everyone feels down sometimes. But when your sadness never goes away, it may be time to seek help.

Coping with Moods

are often accompanied by distinct symptoms (see "Determining Depression" on page 95).

Teens who are depressed may also show other warning signs. Problems at school, defiance, and even criminal behavior are red flags. Some teens even turn to drugs, alcohol, or sexual promiscuity to avoid the feelings of depression. When kids are depressed, their world looks bleak, so they just don't care.

Adolescent depression is increasing at an alarming rate. Recent surveys indicate that as many as one in eight teens suffer from clinical depression. Whatever the cause—society, social changes, increased pressure, unstable environments, or chemical imbalances in the brain—it is a serious problem that can't be ignored.

If you think that your blue moods are more than just the blues, *it is extremely important that you seek and receive prompt professional treatment* (see chapter 6). Depression, if left untreated, can become life threatening.

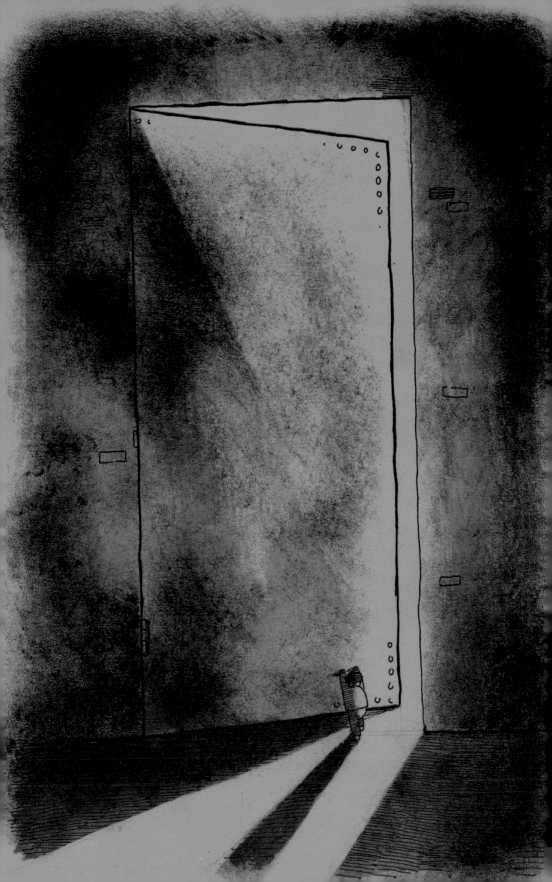

6

BEYOND THE COASTER:
When Moods Become
Mental Illness

Dear Diary,

I can't seem to get it together anymore. I've tried everything: positive thinking, exercise, and even going out more. Nothing seems to make a difference. I'm still down. I don't even enjoy things I used to love.

Then there's the physical stuff. I can't sleep. I'm tired all the time. (That makes me grouchy. My poor family!) I can't think straight. (My grades are suffering!) And don't even mention my weight. (It's soaring.) The more pounds I gain, the more discouraged I feel, and the more dis-

*couraged I feel, the more I eat. The more I eat, the more weight I gain.…
It's hopeless. I feel like I'm trapped.*

When will this ever let up? It's been months! I hate who I'm becoming and I hate what I'm doing to everybody around me. I'm a lousy sister, daughter, and friend. I mess up everything. Sometimes I feel so useless I actually think about running my car into a tree. Is that crazy or what?

Clearly, Carrie is struggling with much more than typical teenage blues. In her case, melancholy has evolved into clinical depression. Her mood has quietly transformed into mental illness.

Mental illness is a "catch-all" term for any disease, imbalance, or defect of the brain that causes thought and behavior disturbances to such a degree that one's ability to cope with ordinary life is compromised. These disturbances can range from mild to severe.

Not everyone suffering from a mental illness is "crazy." In fact, most are high-functioning individuals, and they're all around us. According to the National Institute of Mental Health, an estimated 57 million Americans suffer from various mental disorders in a given year! You probably know at least one or two of them.

Carrie's diary entry is full of clues that she has a serious mental problem: physical symptoms, suicidal thoughts, even the prolonged period over which she's suffered. They're all classic symptoms of depressive illness. She needs professional help.

Unfortunately, unless Carrie has a particularly perceptive family or friend, she'll likely flounder for months, even years, in this condition. Most teens do. They (and many adults in their lives) chalk up extreme blues, fears, or anger to other extreme emotions of adolescence. For some, that works out. For others, the delay is deadly. Each year almost 5,000 young people ages fifteen to twenty-four kill themselves. Carrie could be 5,001.

Coping with Moods

A psychological disorder does not mean you're crazy. It does mean you need to get help.

Moods or Mental Illness?

Emotional outbursts and mood swings are part of adolescence, right? So how do we tell if what we're experiencing is normal or "mental"? Keep in mind that diagnosing mental illness comes down to a question of degree. For example, everyone encounters a sad day, but most people don't have that day stretch into unrelenting months of despair.

Keep in mind that mental disorders are common, particularly less severe ones, and many people suffer with more than

Teen moodiness is often confused with more serious psychological problems.

Coping with Moods

SANE STATS

- More than 26 percent of Americans eighteen or older have diagnosable mental conditions each year.
- About 9.5 of Americans eighteen or older have a mood disorder each year.
- About 6.7 percent of U.S. adults have major depressive disorder (acute, shorter-term depression).
- About 1.5 percent of American adults will experience dysthymic disorder (chronic, mild depression for at least two years) each year.
- About 18 percent of American adults ages eighteen or older have some form of anxiety disorder in any given year.
- About 2.7 percent of Americans eighteen or older have panic disorders.

one at a time. According to the National Institute of Mental Health, an estimated 26 percent of Americans eighteen and older are plagued by diagnosable mental illness in any given year. That means that for every five people you know, one of them probably struggles with psychological problems. Such disorders are common.

With more than 200 classified forms of mental illness, a specific diagnosis can be tricky. The good news is there are widely recognized, additional symptoms (besides mood or feelings) that, when taken as a whole, become solid indicators of a mental disorder. Each disorder has its own set of symptoms. Not surprisingly, some overlap.

COMMON PSYCHOLOGICAL DISORDERS

- major depressive disorder (acute short-term depression)
- dysthymic disorder (long-term mild depression)
- bipolar (manic-depressive) disorder
- anxiety disorders, panic disorders
- obsessive-compulsive disorder (OCD)
- generalized anxiety disorder (GAD)
- social phobia
- specific (or simple) phobias

Let's look at Carrie again. What were the clues that led us to believe she wasn't just "down," but clinically depressed? Here are the most common symptoms of depression. You decide if Carrie fits the description.

- prolonged sadness or depressed mood for apparently no reason
- feeling tired all the time
- lack of energy or enthusiasm
- inability to enjoy things that used to bring pleasure
- irritability
- inability to concentrate

Coping with Moods

- significant weight gain or loss
- change in sleep patterns (inability to fall asleep, stay asleep, or wake)
- feelings of worthlessness or guilt
- thoughts of death or suicide
- digestive disturbances

If someone is experiencing five or more of these symptoms for a period of two weeks or longer, that person is probably

If you feel tired all the time, if everything seems boring, if you just don't feel like doing much of anything, you may be experiencing a depressive disorder.

depressed. Carrie clearly is. And if she honestly evaluated her symptoms, she would know that hers are more than the blues. (For more detailed information about depression and other depressive illnesses, see chapter 5.)

Outward signs of significant psychological issues are often behavioral. Individuals with mental illness can even exhibit disruptive ANTISOCIAL BEHAVIORS, but most don't go that far. Many people with mental disorders become extremely withdrawn, less talkative, or quiet. Others avoid social situations altogether. Still others have frequent, chronic, and extreme shifts in mood or energy. (For example, they may have outbursts of anger, followed by crying, then a whirlwind of activity, followed by extreme lethargy.) Remember, the difference between normal mood swings and possible illness comes down to intensity, frequency, and length of time.

Dear Diary,

I'm really worried about Garrett. All I know is that he's been acting really weird lately. Last week he didn't want to do anything. He couldn't even drag himself to school! And this week, he can't slow down. He never stops talking, he's buying out Sports Authority, and he's up all hours of the night. It's like he's on a permanent caffeine high! Something's really wrong. I never know what to expect. Should I talk to Mom or Dad about it? Maybe he's doing drugs.

Jordan has every right to be concerned about his brother. Note the extremity of Garrett's behaviors. He's not just having a high-energy day, then a week later, a low-energy day. His "moods" are sustained for longer periods of time than what most people experience, and change more frequently with greater contrast and intensity. He's like a pendulum swinging ever higher and higher.

BIPOLAR DISORDER

SYMPTOMS OF MANIA	SYMPTOMS OF DEPRESSION
• racing speech • racing thoughts • decreased need for sleep • increased physical and mental activity • reckless behavior like excessive spending • elevated mood and exaggerated optimism • poor judgment • excessive irritability, impatience, and aggression	• disinterest • prolonged sadness • irritability • fatigue • lack of energy • feelings of worthlessness • sleeping too much • inability to sleep • weight gain or loss • inability to concentrate • loss of enjoyment • thoughts of suicide

Garrett is not just moody. He's actually suffering from a serious, depressive illness called bipolar disorder. You might also have heard of it as manic depression, bipolar affective disorder, or bipolar mood disorder. This disorder reveals itself in recurring episodes of highs (mania) and lows (depression). These episodes aren't the normal periods of happiness and sadness we all experience. They're unpredictable severe shifts that last for weeks or months.

A person with a bipolar disorder may seem to have two "faces"—a happy one and a sad one.

Coping with Moods

How can you tell the difference between mood and mental illness? As with depression, it comes down to discerning degree or intensity. Look at how Jordan describes Garrett. Now look at the symptoms listed below. You be the psychiatrist. What would you conclude?

The difference between bipolar mood disorder and other depressive disorders (like clinical depression) is the manic phase. The person with bipolar disorder often swings between two extremes.

Although mood disorders are widespread—about 9.5 percent of people in the United States alone have some form of mood disorder—only 2.6 percent of those people have bona fide bipolar disorder.

GENIUS AND MADNESS

For many sufferers, the manic phase of bipolar disorder offers prolonged periods of intense productivity and creativity. Some of humanity's greatest minds (and their greatest achievements) were byproducts of this illness. Here are a few:

Abraham Lincoln
Winston Churchill
Ernest Hemingway
Charles Dickens
Ludwig van Beethoven
Sir Isaac Newton
Vincent van Gogh

Warning Signs

In trying to illustrate the differences between mood and mental illness, we've looked at specific symptoms of two disorders: depression and bipolar disorder. We also established that the line between normalcy and illness is sometimes vague and must be determined by degree. Beyond the degrees of intensity, duration, and frequency with which one suffers symptoms, here are some general signs or "red flags" for which we can look that might indicate a need for professional help:

- prolonged sadness or irritability
- confused thinking
- excessive fears
- unjustified worry or anxiety
- social withdrawal
- inability to cope with day-to-day living
- significant changes in sleeping patterns
- dramatic changes in eating habits
- substantial weight gain or loss
- denial of obvious circumstances or problems
- numerous unexplained physical ailments
- suicidal or other violent thoughts
- intense rages
- defiance of authority or criminal behavior
- delusions or hallucinations
- substance abuse

If you experience a few or many of these symptoms, you should probably seek counseling. You're not experiencing simple, adolescent moodiness. It's okay to ask for help.

Where Can I Find Help?

Start with your family physician or other medical professional. You want to rule out other possible physical causes for your symptoms. Your doctor or nurse practitioner can listen to your symptoms and suggest the type of help you need. Here are a few other suggestions for where you might seek help:

· your local health department's mental health division (these services are state funded)

When you're seeking help, your school counselor may be a good place to begin.

TYPES OF MENTAL HEALTH PROFESSIONALS

PSYCHIATRIST: medical doctor with special training in the diagnosis and treatment of mental and emotional illnesses. Like other doctors, psychiatrists are qualified to prescribe medication.

Qualifications: should have a state license and be board eligible or certified by the American Board of Psychiatry and Neurology.

CHILD/ADOLESCENT PSYCHIATRIST: medical doctor with special training in the diagnosis and treatment of mental and emotional illness and behavior problems in children. Child/adolescent psychiatrists are qualified to prescribe medication.

Qualifications: should have a state license and be board eligible or certified by the American Board of Psychiatry and Neurology.

DEVELOPMENTAL BEHAVIORAL PEDIATRICIAN: medical doctor with special training in diagnosis and treatment of mental and emotional illness and behavioral problems in children. Like other doctors, these specialized pediatricians are qualified to prescribe medication.

Qualifications: should have a state license and be board certified in Pediatrics and Developmental Behavioral Pediatrics by the American Board of Pediatrics.

PSYCHOLOGIST: counselor with an advanced degree from an accredited graduate program in psychology, and two or more years of supervised work experience. They are trained to make diagnoses and provide individual and group therapy.

Qualifications: a state license.

MARITAL AND FAMILY THERAPIST: a counselor with a master's degree, with special education and training in marital and family

therapy. Trained to diagnose and provide individual and group counseling.

Qualifications: state license.

CLINICAL SOCIAL WORKER: counselor with a master's degree in social work from an accredited graduate program. Trained to make diagnoses and provide individual and group counseling.

Qualifications: state license; may be a member of the Academy of Certified Social Workers.

LICENSED PROFESSIONAL COUNSELOR: counselor with a master's degree in psychology, counseling, or a related field. Trained to diagnose and provide individual and group counseling.

Qualifications: state license.

MENTAL HEALTH COUNSELOR: counselor with a master's degree and several years of supervised clinical work experience. Trained to diagnose and provide individual and group counseling.

Qualifications: certification by the National Academy of Certified Clinical Mental Health Counselors.

CERTIFIED ALCOHOL AND DRUG ABUSE COUNSELOR: counselor with specific clinical training in alcohol and drug abuse. Trained to diagnose and provide individual and group counseling.

Qualifications: state license.

NURSE PSYCHOTHERAPIST: a registered nurse who is trained in the practice of psychiatric and mental health nursing. Trained to diagnose and provide individual and group counseling. Also some Pediatric Nurse Practitioners work in developmental pediatrics and can prescribe medications under the supervision of a physician.

Qualifications: certification, state license.

PASTORAL COUNSELOR: clergy with training in clinical pastoral education. Trained to diagnose and provide individual and group counseling.

Qualifications: Certification from the American Association of Pastoral Counselors.

- family services agencies (for example, family services, Catholic charities, Jewish social services)
- school counselors
- marriage, family, or child guidance counselors
- therapists: psychologists, or social workers
- psychiatrists
- psychiatric hospitals (some handle psychiatric emergencies)
- clergy (your pastor, minister, rabbi, or priest)

Someone with depressive disorders should see a doctor who has the ability to prescribe medication if needed. That qualification wouldn't be necessary for someone with issues that can be resolved with just talk therapy. He or she may only need a licensed therapist. There are many types of mental health professionals and they often work together as a team.

The list of mental health professionals can seem overwhelming. That's why the best plan to begin is with your regular doctor. She can steer you to the most appropriate professionals.

Next, if you can, be patient in the process. Talk to a few different professionals so that you can choose the person that's right for you. Don't be too quick to dismiss a possible therapist. It takes time for you to feel comfortable enough to really open up and establish a rapport. Give it a few weeks.

If you find after two or three sessions that you're not clicking with the doctor you chose, however, find someone else. You aren't obligated to anyone but yourself. Effective treatment is more important at this point than any perceived sense of loyalty. Move on, and keep moving on until you get the help you need. Selecting the right person is key.

Okay, you've got the ball rolling. You recognized there might be problem, you were courageous enough to seek help, you talked with your doctor, and you've found the right therapist. What's next? That's up to you and the therapist. Every counselor is different, but there are universal approaches to therapy itself.

What Happens During Therapy?

First and foremost, everything is confidential. That means anything you say and do in each session can only go as far as you and your therapist. You needn't worry your therapist will tell your parents what you discuss. Therapists, by law, must respect the privacy of their patients. They can't talk about what you've told them unless you give your permission. The only exception is if the therapist thinks you might harm yourself or someone else.

During your first visit your therapist will probably ask you to explain, in general terms, what's been going on (emotions, actions, circumstances, etc.). If you're meeting with a medical doctor, he will likely discuss medication options and make recommendations. He might even prescribe something then and there. If he does, it's critical to get started on the medication as soon as possible and follow the prescribed treatment exactly, just as you would with an antibiotic for an infection. Some medications take time to work and may require dosing adjustments. It is very important that you do not suddenly discontinue a medication as that can cause withdrawal side effects. Make sure you communicate clearly with your physician so your questions and concerns are addressed.

Your therapist will also probably talk about what to expect in upcoming sessions and suggest how frequently you should meet. (This can be as little as once a month or as often as three times per week.) Be honest about what you can afford time-wise and money-wise.

Whatever you decide, it's important that you stick to the schedule on which you mutually agreed. Don't skip your ap-

If a person with a psychological disorder sees a psychiatrist or other medical professional, she may prescribe medication as part of the individal's treatment.

pointments. Otherwise you may not have enough time with your therapist to work out the problems at hand.

Because every person is different and every situation is unique, therapists have a variety of treatments in their medical bag of tricks. They may choose to use one kind of therapy with you, or they may think it beneficial to combine different types (for example, using medication with talk therapy). Therapeutic strategies can include several techniques.

Relaxation Training

Here the therapist teaches her patients to relax their minds and bodies—in all situations—so they can better cope with daily living.

Stress Management

In this type of therapy, people learn the signs of stress and ways to deal with it.

Cognitive-Behavioral Therapy

This kind of therapy helps people identify negative patterns of thinking, and then teaches them specific methods for transforming such thoughts into positive or constructive thinking. (We talked about this a lot in chapter 1.)

Many treatment programs for psychological disorders involve some form of "talk therapy."

No matter what approach the therapist takes, he will monitor your progress to see if the strategy is working. If you're uncomfortable with the therapy or the therapist, be sure to tell your parents. If you feel that therapy isn't helping you, don't be afraid to try a different therapist or a different kind of therapy.

Accepting Your Feelings

If you suspect that the moods you're experiencing are something more than just moods, the first step is to seek help. The second step is to accept your feelings. Despite the wide range of mental illnesses, most people share similar experiences along the way. You might initially deny or ignore the warning signs, afraid of what others will think. You also struggle with the "Why me?" question, wondering what triggered your illness or what's wrong with you. You might even fear being labeled or stigmatized. These are all normal responses.

Many mental illnesses are symptoms of brain malfunction. There's absolutely no shame in that. Most sufferers can't help their illness. It's not "you" or anything you're doing or not doing. Like diabetes or heart disease, many brain disorders are physiologically based. There's no one to blame. It just is.

Educate Yourself

There's nothing wrong with asking for help when you need it. In fact, it takes a lot of courage to do so. Seeking solutions to your problems instead of wallowing in them (or allowing them to worsen) is a mark of maturity.

Instead of fearing your illness, find out all you can about it. That's empowering. Then share what you learn with others close to you. Information will help them better understand what you're going through, and you won't feel quite as isolated.

With treatment, many people with mental disorders, from mild to severe, return to functional, productive, and fulfilling lives.

Dear Diary,

I'm really having a problem with Mom getting married again. I don't know ... Henry's a nice guy and all. It's just that no one can ever replace Dad. Maybe I need help. I should be over this by now. He died five years ago—but it seems like only yesterday he was swingin' me dizzy in the back yard. I really miss him. It hurts so bad.

Even if you're not severely ill, therapy can have many benefits. Most people learn a lot about themselves and grow as individuals. They also discover ways of coping with difficult situations that they may not have encountered before. Even more emerge more confident and self-assured. Seeking help is not a sign of weakness—it's a sign of strength!

Further Reading

Barrick, Marilyn C. *Emotions: Transforming Anger, Fear and Pain—Creating Heart-Centeredness in a Turbulent World*. Corwin Springs, Mont.: Summit University Press, 2002.

Brinkerhoff, Shirley. *Drug Therapy and Anxiety Disorders*. Philadelphia, Penn.: Mason Crest Publishers, 2004.

Esherick, Joan. *Drug Therapy and Mood Disorders*. Philadelphia, Penn.: Mason Crest Publishers, 2004.

Greenfield, Susan. *The Private Life of the Brain: Emotions, Consciousness, and the Secret of the Self*. New York: John Wiley, 2000.

Kindlon, Daniel James. *Raising Cain: Protecting the Emotional Life of Boys*. New York: Ballantine Books, 2011.

Libal, Autum. *Runaway Train: Youth with Emotional Disturbance*. Philadelphia, Penn.: Mason Crest Publishers, 2004.

Mosatche, Harriet S. *Too Old for This, Too Young for That! Your Survival Guide for the Middle School Years*. Minneapolis, Minn.: Free Spirit Publishing, 2000.

Sichel, Deborah. *Women's Moods: What Every Woman Must Know about Hormones, the Brain, and Emotional Health*. New York: William Morrow, 2013.

For More Information

The Centers for Disease Control and Prevention
www.cdc.gov

Family Education
www.familyeducation.com

Focus Adolescent Services
www.focusas.com/EmotionalHealth.html

The Nemours Foundation
www.kidshealth.com

Bad Moods
endoflifecare.tripod.com/kidsyoungadults/id43.html

Web MD
www.webmd.com

Palo Alto Medical Foundation
www.pamf.org/teen/life

Teen Moods and Support Groups
psychcentral.com

Publisher's note:
The websites listed on these pages were active at the time of publication. The publisher is not responsible for websites that have changed their addresses or discontinued operation since the date of publication. The publisher will review and update the websites upon each reprint.

Glossary

ADRENAL GLANDS A pair of glands that produces, among other things, hormones.

ANTISOCIAL BEHAVIORS Actions, usually harmful, that are contrary to those accepted by society.

ATYPICAL Opposite of what is expected or usual.

BIOCHEMICAL The chemical characteristic of a living organism.

CAPITALIZING Gaining by turning something into an advantage.

CEREBRAL Relating to the brain or the intellect.

CHRONICALLY Appearing for an extended time or frequently recurring.

CLINICAL DEPRESSION Depression that is diagnosable through observation.

COGNITIVE Relating to the process of knowing.

CYNICS People who believe that human conduct is based on self-interest, and who find fault with everyone and everything.

DIAGNOSTIC THRESHOLDS Established levels of what is considered "normal" or at what point intervention is needed.

DIFFUSED Not concentrated; to break up.

DISPROPORTIONATE Being out of relationship with the amount expected.

ENTITLEMENT Having the right to something.

EUPHORIA A feeling of extreme joy.

EVOLVE To develop, mature.

FLUCTUATING To shift back and forth.

HORMONES A substance in the body that produces an effect on the activity of specific cells.

HYPOTHALAMUS A part of the brain that produces releasing hormones and regulates the body's water balance, temperature, and appetite.

INTERPERSONAL Involving relationships between people.

LETHARGY Abnormal tiredness.

METABOLISM The chemical changes in the body that provide the energy for vital processes and activity.

NEUROTRANSMITTERS Substances that send nerve impulses across the synapses.

PASSIVE-AGGRESSIVE A kind of interaction whereby someone reacts in an uncooperative manner to the expectations of another without expressing hostility openly or actively.

PATHOLOGICAL Habitual and compulsive behavior that is altered or caused by disease.

PERVASIVE Spreading throughout.

PREFRONTAL CORTEX The part of the brain responsible for thinking, expression of personality, and acting in socially acceptable ways.

PSYCHOSOCIAL Interaction between a person and society.

PUBERTAL HORMONES Hormones that are released in the body that bring about puberty, usually between ages nine and sixteen in girls, and between thirteen and fifteen in boys.

SUBJECTIVE Modified or affected by personal views.

SURVIVAL MECHANISMS Bodily functions or instincts, such as the fight-or-flight mechanism, that exist to aid the body in surviving.

WESTERN CIVILIZATION stemming from Greco-Roman traditions; usually considered to be Europe and the United States.

Index

Picture Credits

Artville pp. 40, 86, 116, 117
BrandX pp. 13, 15
EyeWire pp. 83, 111
iDream pp. 26, 44, 62, 74, 84, 108
Image Source pp. 21, 78, 94, 96, 102
Johan Reineke | Dreamstime.com: p. 36
LifeART p. 10
Lucian Milasan | Dreamstime.com: p. 53
Masterseries pp. 28, 80, 90, 98
PhotoAlto pp. 33, 47, 71, 101, 105
Photodisc pp. 16, 39, 50, 55, 58, 65, 68

The individuals in these images are models, and the images are for illustrative purposes only.

To the best knowledge of the publisher, all other images are in the public domain. If any image has been inadvertantly uncredited or miscredited, please notify Vestal Creative Services, Vestal, New York 13850, so that rectification can be made for future printings.

Biographies

Jean Ford is a freelance author, writer, award-winning illustrator, and public speaker. Internationally recognized, her work includes writing for periodicals from the United States to China, and speaking to audiences from as close as her tri-state area to as far away as Africa. Although she generally writes and speaks on nonfiction topics, Jean also enjoys writing and illustrating children's books.

Carolyn Bridgemohan, MD, is a senior staff member of the Developmental Medicine Center, Children's Hospital, Boston, and instructor of pediatrics at Harvard Medical School, Boston. She specializes in assessment and treatment of autism and developmental disorders in young children. Her clinical practice includes children and youth with autism, hearing impairment, developmental language disorders, global delays, mental retardation, and attention and learning disorders. Dr. Bridgemohan is coeditor of "Bright Futures: Case Studies for Primary Care Clinicians: Child Development and Behavior," a curriculum used nationwide in pediatric residency training programs.

Dr. Sara Forman is a board certified physician in Adolescent Medicine. She has worked at Bentley Student Health Services since 1995 as a Senior Consulting Physician. Dr. Forman graduated from Barnard College and Harvard Medical School and completed her residency in Pediatrics at Children's Hospital of Philadelphia. After completing a fellowship in Adolescent Medicine at Children's Hospital Boston (CHB), she became an attending physician in that division. Dr. Forman's specialties include general adolescent health and eating disorders. She is the Director of the Outpatient Eating Disorders Program at Children's Hospital in Boston. In addition to seeing students at Bentley College, Dr. Forman sees primary care adolescent patients in the Adolescent Clinic at Children's and at The Germaine Lawrence School, a residential school for emotionally disturbed teenage girls.